The Miracle Goes On

by John W. Peterson
with Richard Engquist

OF THE ZONDERVAN CORPORATION | GRAND RAPIDS, MICHIGAN 49506

THE MIRACLE GOES ON

Grand Rapids, Michigan

Fifth printing May 1977

Library of Congress Cataloging in Publication Data

Peterson, John W
The miracle goes on.
1. Peterson, John W. 2. Gospel musicians—Correspondence, reminiscences, etc. I. Engquist, Richard, joint author. II. Title.
ML410.P2957A3 783.7 76-4976

Printed in the United States of America

Contents

Dear John,

To use one of your phrases, this lyric "took shape" in my mind while I was working on the new draft of your story. Obviously, it's an attempt to put into verse form some of the highlights of your life . . . from the point of view of one who looks at you with admiration and deep affection!

—RICHARD ENGQUIST

I saw a cross, Perfection on it bleeding.
I saw my sin, for I'd not walked His way.
I saw His tears, His blood which was my ransom –
He took my heart and washed my guilt away.

That was a miracle to me.
My life redeemed, my soul set free.
And since that day, through many a gray and golden year
The miracle goes on.

I heard Him call and ask for my obedience.
My stubborn will resisted for a time.
The battle raged, but then when I surrendered,
He gave me joy surpassingly sublime.

That was a miracle to me –
His chains of love that set me free!
Complete submission to His sovereign will – and still
The miracle goes on.

I suffered pain, resentment, and injustice;
He showed me envy, vanity, and pride!
Confessed my sin and prayed for my tormentors –
He gave me peace and brushed my tears aside.

That was a miracle to me –
The death of pride that set me free.
For Jesus' love remains when earthly hope is gone.
The miracle goes on.

I looked at death in puzzlement and wonder –
Beyond the grave I saw the Savior smile.
I cast aside all worldly plans and pleasures;
He stayed death's hand for yet a little while.

That was a miracle to me!
My every moment His shall be –
The past, the present, and the future free from fear!
The miracle goes on!

The Miracle Goes On

1

Boca Raton, Florida – January 10, 1975

Throughout my hurried supper the melodies keep ringing in my mind.

Jesus is calling America – calling her back to the fold;
Jesus is calling America – calling the young and the old.
Back to the "faith of our fathers," faith we need in
these troubled days;
Jesus is calling America . . .

Strange perhaps, but that's how the Lord made me, so that even years from now when the text may be fuzzy or lost to memory, the tune will still be fresh in my mind. The harmonies will fall into place and the orchestration will be as crystal clear as it was when I heard it this afternoon in rehearsal.

Strange, because the *text* is paramount: the music is meant to serve it. Music touches the emotions, but there's only one way to get a message across — if you *do* get it across — to the mind and will of man: through words. Sometimes a wordless melody will take form in my mind, but if it becomes a song I shape the tune to enhance the text, not vice versa. I've got something I want to say, something I believe the Lord wants me to say, and songs are my medium of communication. Nevertheless, no matter how appealing a melody I create, if the words don't come through, I've failed.

I learned that long ago as a teen-ager back in Wichita, Kansas, when Haldor Lillenas, a fine old gospel songwriter, came to town to lead the music in an evangelistic crusade. For once my desire to learn about songwriting overcame my diffidence. I screwed up my courage, telephoned, and asked him for an interview.

Fearful and hopeful, I approached that venerable Norwegian gentleman, a sheaf of manuscript paper under my arm. I can still see him adjusting his glasses, hear him humming through my tunes. Finally he said, "I want to give you some advice, young man. The most important part of a song is the lyric. Be very careful with your lyric. Go through it again and again until it's the best you can make it. Until it says something and is poetic."

Says something.

Yes, and something that squares with Scripture. God took the trouble to communicate with us in concrete ideas. Whatever we need to know about Him and about ourselves is set forth clearly in His Word. A gospel song may or may not break new ground or introduce new concepts. It may be a paraphrase. But it *can't* distort biblical truth. I am under obligation to communicate the gospel as much as the man in the pulpit. It's not a question of simply writing pretty verses.

Some people will find this definition too rigid, but it's a concept I have held throughout my life as a songwriter. Many songs today deal with spiritual matters — attractive songs, effective songs — perhaps even speaking of Jesus, but in such a vague, sentimental, or wishy-washy way that there's no tie-in to sound doctrine, to His great work of salvation, redemption, and sanctification. Such compositions, however compelling they may be on an emotional level, do not qualify in my mind as gospel songs.

Dogmatic? Maybe. But this attitude is born out of a feeling of responsibility to make the gospel message clear and plain, to set forth biblical truth precisely. Even in a song which deals primarily with personal experience, I feel obliged to relate that experience to sound doctrine.

I gulp down the last of my meal, for time is racing by.

This afternoon's rehearsal lasted four hours — longer than anyone planned. Putting together the choir with the orchestra and soloists in one afternoon is no mean task, even when many are professionals. Throughout the rehearsal a distracting hum of activity goes on all around that has nothing to do with the message or the music — except that it does. Light men are busily working out levels and intensities, mixing colors, trying a dimmer here or a spotlight there. The sound system presents its own problems and challenges, and the sound engineers have their hands full, especially in a big auditorium like Bibletown Community Church.

Everyone pushes hard at a moment like this: singers, instrumentalists, technical crew. *They're Your people, Lord, and they know their jobs. But in the final analysis, they're trusting You to make something wonderful happen, if it be Your will.*

How many times have I been through a week like this? The excitement of preparing a major work for its world premiere dwarfs every other experience in a composer's life. At the beginning I feel as if we're standing at the bottom of Mount Everest, and after the first choir rehearsal I wonder if we will ever make it to the top — despair mingled with anticipation; hope with hopelessness.

The week passes, and bit by bit things start to take shape. I meet the orchestra for the first time and discover that my conducting score is a shambles, a rush copying job full of omissions and mistakes. I'll have to keep all the corrections in my mind. The performance is tonight, and it's far too late to make a new copy.

A wave of bone-weariness washes over me as I hurry from the dining hall to my bedroom. I wish I had an hour for a nap. Tomorrow morning I'll feel drained, when tonight's exhilaration and spiritual uplift have faded to an afterglow. I make a mental note to have breakfast at 8:00 rather than 7:30, but there's no time now to dwell on tomorrow's timetable. I have to get into my black suit and over to the auditorium.

As I quickly change clothes, I'm grateful for the air conditioner in my room. Florida is warm even in January, and a clammy, invisible mist in the air outside makes breathing difficult for those of us who thrive on the dust-dry atmosphere of the desert.

It's time to pray to the God who watches o'er us;
It's time to seek His help without delay . . .

Was there ever a time which was not "a time to pray"? I doubt it. But tonight I'm praying with an increased sense of urgency, wanting so much to do my part in a special way for the Lord who is my life and for the nation that nurtured me.

I'm praying for myself, too. Why hide it? It's a scary moment for an artist when one of his works is judged by the public for the first time. So much of the person has gone into it; so many high hopes are bound up in it; so much time and effort and money are invested in it that the event assumes an importance it probably shouldn't have.

By now I should know myself pretty well — should be honest enough to own up to the carnal need for approval and acceptance which throughout my life has been lurking behind my desire to serve God and sometimes threatening to supplant it. The past few years have brought me more in the way of adulation and rewards than most people ever know. Perhaps more than anyone should know for the good of his soul. I've tried to keep it all in perspective, to acknowledge every day my dependence on the Lord, along with a constantly renewed sense of surprise and thanksgiving for the abundance of His blessings.

What an amazing bundle of contradictions is a human being! When God made us in His image, He certainly didn't make us simple; and when man fell from grace, he only added to the complexity. I praise the Lord that on Calvary He dealt for eternity with my nature. Praise Him that at the time of my rebirth He accepted me as I was and took over the reins of my life, knowing full well how often I would stumble and falter. Praise Him again that He has guided me faithfully and forgivingly through every failure and mistake in judgment.

But as long as I'm mortal, I don't kid myself *about* myself. Any competent psychiatrist who took a good look at me would find even now a powerful drive to excel — a human hunger for recognition and success. And tangled up with it, the lingering torment of self-doubt. These twin themes have struggled for dominance all through my life, and God in His mercy has never seen fit to obliterate them.

The Bible puts it very well: the Lord makes us receptacles for living water, but we must never lose sight of the fact that we *are* receptacles — earthen vessels, at that, with flaws, bumps, weak spots, cracks, and imperfections.

I want to glorify You tonight, Lord. If there is living water in this new work, it is of You. Let the people be blessed tonight, and don't let me get in the way. Don't let the music get in the way either.

Music has a power all its own — an almost palpable power. Whether God made us with an implicit ability to respond to rhythm, melody, and form, or whether from the moment of birth we are conditioned for such response, I couldn't say. But there is no denying it is there. We know instinctively that a lullaby will soothe and quiet a crying baby, that a plaintive lament will activate the tear ducts, that the driving rhythm of the Rolling Stones will churn up emotions and set pulses racing. When you deal with music, you play with dynamite. It can inspire or depress, curse or bless.

On a hot August afternoon more than thirty years ago my fellow servicemen and I were put through a forced march with full field packs on our backs. How many miles? — something absurd, designed to push us to the limit of our physical endurance. About halfway through I ran out of water and was "spitting cotton." Dust and sweat trickled down my face in muddy rivulets, and the screaming pain in my muscles had subsided into a constant ache. Then the final insult — an airplane swooped down and gassed us to simulate combat conditions.

Three or four miles from home base we had a rest break. I was sure I would never get up. Fellows were dropping on all sides. An ambulance buzzed around, and the medics were hard-pressed to keep up with the casualties.

Suddenly the post band appeared in full regalia. The thrilling cadences of "The Stars and Stripes Forever" were an injection of adrenalin into bodies far gone in collapse. One moment I was totally spent; the next I was on my feet, renewed, tingling, marching those last few miles back to base courtesy of the genius of John Philip Sousa and the bright, brassy sound of an air force band.

The power of music!

I know what music is capable of doing; know well that people can be manipulated emotionally, fired up to the point of near frenzy or lulled into a somnolent complacency. *Dynamite.*

Long ago as a music student I caught a glimpse of the inherent possibilities in the art form. Aesthetically I realized that music could be an end in itself, but that didn't satisfy me. My professors at the conservatory wanted me to give myself to music. I wanted to give myself to God. The gospel was my driving force, and I saw that if I were to be a composer of sacred music who was worthy of the name I would have to be sensitive to God's leading and judicious in my choice of a musical palette. I couldn't do just as I pleased.

True, the whole range of musical expression was there for me to choose from — God had made it so — but at the same time He wanted to guide my hand. I had seen enough of the use of music, even in evangelism, to sense that there was no place the devil wouldn't go to get his hands on this powerful force and twist it to his own ends. People could easily be charged up with a tune and a hypnotic rhythm. To what end? To burnish the ego of the evangelist or song leader — to line his pocketbook? God forbid! The whole point was to prepare an emotional climate wherein people could be open to the message of the gospel — open enough, hearts touched enough, so that they would respond to His call and His claim upon their lives.

* * *

My tie is straight, there's no obvious lint on my tuxedo, and I don't look too tired. That's important to me, perhaps more important than it should be. With a rueful inward smile I glance at the bifocals on my dresser and remember my own vanity. Funny, how I don't like to get up in front of a congregation wearing bifocals. Just as I'd rather nobody knew about the medicine in my dresser drawer, the little bottle of pills that travels with me everywhere in case I have an asthmatic attack.

Is it all vanity, Lord? You know the countless number of times I've felt inadequate, scared, unsure of myself. You know it all, Lord: what a mixed bag of a mortal I am – my frailty, my humanity, my insecurity, and my zeal.

In a little while I'll be on the podium with every eye focused on me. The performers and the audience have a right to trust me, to feel that everything is going smoothly. I would not consciously do anything to cause them anxiety or apprehension. If I felt ill, I'd do everything in my power not to let it show. An earthen vessel, all right, but it wouldn't — couldn't — be a blessing to anyone not to keep the old thing as polished and shiny as possible.

If there's any point, Lord, in sorting out all the motives and rationalizations, You'll have to let me know, and I'll try. But, in the meantime, You've given me a job to do.

This is my job, my calling, my ministry. But in a deeper sense, Lord, it isn't mine at all. You brought it about and affirmed it over and over again. If I've let myself get carried away with a good image, if vanity has shined up my ego too brightly, forgive me – but use me. Tonight belongs to You. This music belongs to You. My whole life belongs to You.

2

When Haldor Lillenas explained to me the crucial importance of the text in a gospel song, he could not have guessed what a lasting impression his words would make. I was an unprepossessing kid, my early efforts at songwriting rudimentary in the extreme. Moreover, our meeting could not have lasted half an hour. Yet I took his advice seriously, and not merely because instinct told me he was right. Lillenas was a man whose personality — glowing with mature faith, a kind of saintliness — left me awestruck. I have known many such individuals, and my reaction is always the same: admiration and awe, with a wistful longing to have some of those saintly qualities myself.

My Grandmother Peterson, for example. Like my other grandparents, she had come to America from Sweden soon after the great mid-nineteenth century wave of immigration. Drawn by the promise of land and the longing for freedom from privation; sometimes driven by a passion for adventure and change; occasionally, I suppose, escaping from personal problems, family difficulties, or disgrace in their homeland, thousands upons thousands of Swedes found their way to the Midwest, from Minnesota's wooded lakes to the Kansas plains, seeking out one another and eventually forming communities which were little bits of Scandinavia transplanted to a new land.

Grandmother Peterson's odyssey to Kansas was interrupted by a stay in Chicago, where fortuitously she came under the ministry of Dwight L. Moody and attended his services at Farwell Hall and at North Side Tabernacle. She knew Moody personally and also became involved in the ministry of Fredrick Franson, the man God used to spark missionary interest among Swedish immigrants and who founded the missionary organization now known as TEAM. Grandmother remained a strong and dedicated Christian all her life.

Sometime after the great Chicago fire she found her way to Kansas and settled in the Swedish settlement in the Smoky River Valley near McPherson. There she met and married a fellow immigrant, Claus Peterson, whose trek from the Old World to the New had been marked by both hazards and opportunities — and who had seized both.

When he and his companions landed in New York, they were met by representatives of the Union Pacific Railroad who were scouting replacements for a crew of section hands on the transcontinental railroad then under construction. Sickness and Indian raids took a heavy toll among construction workers, and the crew my grandfather joined was a replacement for one that had been wiped out in an Indian attack. He and his fellow crewmen worked for some time under the protection of the United States Cavalry, and when the railway was completed, the company rewarded them with land grants in Kansas.

A piece of prairie near McPherson, Kansas, became Claus Peterson's tangible stake in America, and to a log cabin there he brought his bride. Life was rugged, but the land was good, and a growing nation was clamoring for more and more wheat. Sadly, the young couple had hardly begun to carve their niche when the log farmhouse burned to the ground and they had to begin again.

Stern people, those Swedish pioneers, but stalwart. And many of them saintly. A goodly number lived long lives, and happily I came to know some of them when I was a child in the late 1920s.

Supreme among saints of my childhood was Grandfather Nelson. Like many Scandinavian immigrants he was serious-minded, self-controlled, dignified — a kind man, but with an austerity about him and never much emotional display. To me he was an awe-inspiring person. Being in his presence was like being near the Lord.

Three times a day, regardless of who was around, grandfather would go to his desk, pull out his Bible and hymnbook, sing a song and read from the Scriptures, and finally pray — always aloud; always in Swedish; three times a day, every day.

One of my early writing efforts — a very amateurish one — was a song in honor of grandfather's birthday. Three of my older brothers were doing radio broadcasting at the time, and they performed it over the air. It was my first song to be performed publicly, although I didn't think in those terms then.

Whatever its merits, grandfather was impressed. He took me aside and said, "Johann, the Lord is going to use you some day. He will use you and your writing." I paid little attention at the time, but he must have detected the spark of a native gift in me and prayed often that the Lord would develop it.

He was close to God. His thrice-daily devotions, far from being a ritual display, were as natural to grandfather as breathing. It was as if the formal daily periods of prayer and praise were the outward signs of an intimate, endless conversation with God.

Where did it originate, this singular rapport with the Infinite? Apparently the Lord came to grandfather while he was alone, working in the Iowa cornfields. Suddenly the young farmer came under great conviction, and without another soul at hand for counsel or encouragement, he made his decision to live for Christ.

Following his conversion, grandfather moved his growing family to the new state of Kansas which was "dry" while Iowa was "wet." They settled on a 160-acre piece of land midway between the towns of Burdick and Lost Springs, and this became their permanent home.

In Kansas, Charles Nelson became one of the organizers of a Lutheran Church, but soon — perhaps because he sensed a need for services which were less formal and exuded a greater spiritual warmth — he helped to found a Swedish Mission Friends Church. Their meetings were held in a schoolhouse, and for fourteen years grandfather was a prime mover in the church, taking care of the janitorial work, furnishing kerosene for the lamps, serving as Sunday school superintendent and teacher and moderator of the congregation. Even after a church building was erected, the group was frequently without a regular pastor, so grandfather and the other farmers took turns in the pulpit.

As my grandparents grew older, they relinquished the now greatly expanded farm to their children and moved to a house in Lost Springs. There the nine surviving sons and daughters gathered for their parents' golden wedding anniversary to discover that grandfather had a surprise in store for them. Freed from the responsibilities of the farm, he had plunged into a concentrated study of English and was able to give a magnificent extemporaneous talk in the language of the new land.

Four years later grandmother became ill — she was in her seventy-ninth year — and once more the children gathered. My Uncle Charles described the scene:

"Again I was to witness a further demonstration of the courage, fortitude, and faith that had characterized father's life and set him apart, at least to me, from other men. As the moments drew to a close for mother, he virtually bridged the way for her transition from this world into a better and richer life: 'Let not your hearts be troubled . . . ,' Father's voice came unfaltering and clear: 'The Lord is my shepherd; I shall not want.' 'For I am persuaded that neither death, nor life, nor angels, nor principalities, nor things present, nor things to come, nor powers, nor height, nor depth, nor anything else in all creation will be able to separate us from the love of God in Christ Jesus our Lord.' Here faith seemed lost in realization, hope in fruition, but love remaining — the golden link that survives the tomb. And so mother passed away."

Grandfather lived on in the home in Lost Springs with his daughter Hilma. Late in 1939 he became very ill, and my mother, one of my sisters, one of my brothers, and I drove out to see him. He told my mother that the Lord had promised him he would be home by Christmas. Mother began to cry, and he tried to comfort her, for he wanted to go. To him it was nothing but a step from here to glory to be with the Lord. And the Lord had spoken to him audibly, of this he was certain.

A few days before Christmas he got up and dressed as usual, walked from his bedroom into the dining room, sat down for a few seconds, then rose and took a step or two toward the kitchen before falling to the floor. Hilma rushed to his side.

"My time is not up . . . just yet," he whispered.

Later that day he died.

Grandfather Nelson. I see him in all his dignity, faithfully immersed in his devotions. I think about his long life — that unschooled immigrant boy — preaching, praying, playing host to a hundred traveling ministers, building, working, singing, tilling the soil, rearing a family, hoping, holding his beloved wife's hand while she crossed the bridge from life to Life.

And I think about all of his descendants who are Christians, and of all that God has enabled us to be and do. I think about it, and I wonder: how much was a result of his prayers — his untiring, believing prayers?

I think about it, and I'm grateful.

3

Boca Raton . . . 1975

From my room to the church is only a short stroll. The parking lots are already full, and I see drivers circling the area, trying to find spaces. That's encouraging! A warm night, a lovely town, an impressive sanctuary. Nobody could ask for a more agreeable setting. A milling crowd outside the church makes me wonder if the place is already filled.

With a quickening sense of excitement and anticipation I walk past the throng and head for a side door. To my embarrassment I discover that the door is locked and no one is there to let me in. That means the musicians have all taken their places, and it also means I'll have to brave the crowd at the front door. Trying to appear as unobtrusive as possible, I thread through the crowd, and a smiling usher nods me on my way. It's not easy to be inconspicuous when you're a big hulk of a guy in a black tuxedo.

Music drifts up from the organ, and there's a hush of

subdued conversation from the crowd. That's Merrill Dunlop on the organ bench. Don Hustad, another celebrated musician, is in the audience. He has served on our music faculty this week. Merrill and Don have been my friends, models, and inspiration for many years. At times I've looked on them with envy, but always with admiration and appreciation. A special kind of brotherhood exists among church musicians, and my friendship with these two goes way back to my days at Moody.

I was a student at Moody Bible Institute when Merrill Dunlop was organist and music director at the Chicago Gospel Tabernacle. Every Moody student was expected to have a "practical Christian work" assignment in addition to his classwork, and for my assignment I requested a Sunday school class at the tabernacle so I could observe and learn from Merrill. He was, and is, a craftsman who writes beautiful songs — a "musician's composer." His hair is gray now, and there's a slight stoop to his shoulders, but he knows how to make the organ sing as sweetly as ever.

Now I'm at the front of the auditorium among the musicians, where the air of eagerness to "get on with it" is keen. And here are other old friends and associates who have an emotional investment in the occasion.

Torrey Johnson, pastor of Bibletown Church. Don Newman of the Bibletown Conference Center. Torrey and Don have both been intimately associated with the National Church Music Leadership Conference Association, and tonight marks the climax of our sixth annual conference. A lot of music has been made here, but more important, lives have been changed and ministries enhanced.

And here's Pat Zondervan, quietly moving about with a warm smile and a word of encouragement for everyone. *Thank you, Lord, for Pat and all he stands for.* We've knocked heads from time to time over business matters, but he's never let me down or failed to live up to a promise. Tonight means a lot to him, too; he's in it and behind it with all his being.

Pat grips my hand, and I see the familiar look of confidence and enthusiasm in his eyes. He's always there to lift you when you need a lift. Somewhere in my files back home in Arizona is a stack of letters from Pat, written over the years, each one with a note of prayerful optimism — some explicit personal affirmation. We've been through fire and glory together, and he means the world to me.

The presence of people like these seems like a kind of seal on my life, and I thank God for it. Not pride, exactly, but the warm feeling that comes from achievement and having people you admire and respect share it with you.

I'm getting edgy. I want to say, "Come on, Torrey, let's go." My fatigue is forgotten, and I'm on fire to get started. A conductor has to embody excitement. The other musicians must see it in your eyes, sense it in your posture. At best the audience picks it up, too, and the atmosphere becomes electric.

Merrill has finished the organ prelude, and Torrey gets up to welcome the crowd. A gasp of surprise sweeps through the building when he reports that between five and six hundred people have had to be turned away. Every seat in the auditorium is filled — 2200 people. I can't help wishing I could expand the walls so those others could get in. I hope they'll try again tomorrow evening when the concert is repeated. My heart swells a bit, and on second thought maybe it *is* pride. Nobody's immune.

I glance across the platform to Don Wyrtzen at the piano and know he feels it, too. Don's face is glowing — as it should be — but there are signs of strain as well. He's been pushing himself too hard. We've all been pushing him. If he didn't have so many gifts, perhaps we wouldn't expect so much of him or make so many demands.

Don came to work with me when I was president of Singspiration. He brought a freshness to the company that was inspiring. I sensed the talent behind his shy smile, sensed the hand of God on him, and felt he would become an outstanding composer and arranger. Tonight I know that my expectations have been fulfilled. This new musical is a collaboration between

Don and me. For several years he has done my orchestrations, but this time his creativity has gone into the mix in a new way. I've never tried this before, working with another composer on a major musical. Maybe it won't happen again, but I know it was right this time. It was also good for my ego to be subjected to the discipline of sharing in the creation of a large-scale work.

Don's father, Jack Wyrtzen, is in the audience. I can only imagine the pride and happiness he must feel. Probably no one listening will be able to guess which melodies are mine and which are Don's; we don't identify them in the program. Hopefully it will sound of one piece — a joining of forces and not a competition. If it doesn't come off, we'll soon know it. And we'll have to answer for it, too, to a demanding public.

That's an occupational hazard in a calling like mine. When you produce a work that stirs a response in people's hearts, when it gives them inspiration or some measure of comfort and assurance, they listen to your next work with heightened expectations.

God has poured out blessings on my compositions over the years, and nobody knows better than I that with the acceptance of each new piece something beyond it will be expected the next time. There's no way to rest on past laurels.

This could be a terrible burden if it were not for three crucial factors.

First, I never think of the work as my exclusive property. In a real sense it's not my property at all. In yielding my life to God and attempting each day to renew that sense of dependence, I find I can trust Him to have His way — to produce fruit, if that is His will, or to let some effort go unnoticed.

Second, a composer never stops learning. Each composition stretches me further, giving me a richer palette, as a painter might express it. The music I write today I could not have written twenty years ago, or ten, or perhaps even five. As the creative horizons expand, there is an ever-enlarging variety of possibilities.

Third, the people who come to hear my music are with me

from the start. They come eagerly, expecting a blessing. Oh, I have critics — severe ones, and plenty of them — but they don't show up at a John Peterson concert. Their pot shots are taken from the sidelines, and I'm glad of it.

Come to think of it, does that really make my job less demanding? Maybe the most difficult challenge is to fulfill the expectations of an admirer. I look out over the crowd and wonder.

4

Kansas wheat fields have their own peculiar beauty, and most people who grow up close to the soil become inbued with the rhythm of the seasons and the natural, but somehow mysterious, process of planting, growth, harvest, and rest. There are others, however, whose nature seems to defy their origins and who go through life like displaced persons. Restless, unsatisfied, always looking for greener pastures — out of rhythm and fated for perpetual frustration.

My father was such a man. He was reared as a farm boy, and for more than twenty years after he and mother married he continued to live on the land at various periods without finding fulfillment in it. Even when he farmed, he never became a farmer.

His father, Grandfather Peterson, had upon retirement "divvied up" the land among his sons in eighty-acre tracts. Uncle Fred and Uncle Gust labored hard and serenely, but dad was an alien among the cows and the cornfields. He was here, there, and everywhere, putting down fragile roots for a few months or years at a time, then pulling them up and moving on.

His heart was in building. Though he had little formal education, he possessed a natural gift for designing and constructing buildings. Many homes in the area were products of his creativity. He would envision the finished structure in his mind, dash off a few sketches, then set about building it. He worked furiously, and when he was hammering away at a project the other workers grumbled that nobody could keep up such a pace.

A brilliant man, a dreamer, full of grand designs beyond realization. Who knows what Ephraim Peterson might have become with a good education and the right doors open to him. An architect? An engineer?

But maybe not. Maybe he would always have been just what he was: a man whose schemes far outdistanced his ability to bring them to a practical, satisfactory conclusion.

His grain door, for example — a pot of gold which appeared, beckoned enticingly, then faded away. One of the large railroad companies needed a new design for the door on its grain car; they advertised for a new design, promising that whoever came up with the right one would be rewarded with the princely sum of one million dollars.

My father got busy and designed a door. Other men were involved as well; whether they financed his working model or built it to his specifications, I don't know. When railroad officials inspected my father's invention, they offered him $200,000 for it.

A fortune — but not the million dollars that had been promised, and dad stubbornly resisted. Weeks dragged by, then months, and at last the company bought another design. Dad's great plan had come to nothing.

A dreamer, yes. Maybe something of a genius. But a nomad. He moved his expanding family from house to house, area to area. Sometimes the children would begin a school term in one state and complete it in another. Mother must have found this difficult. Undoubtedly it was unsettling for the children as well, though they recall it philosophically and without resentment. Mother had her hands full: Rudy had been born in 1901, and the next eight years saw the addition of two brothers, Bob and Bill, and two sisters, Mabel and Marie. Then there was a gap of six years before the advent of Ken, and another six-year gap before I — very much the baby of the family — came along on November 1, 1921.

Dad's restlessness and frequent moves were mitigated by the fact that the family was loving and close-knit. Mother's devotion to the Lord went deep, and though dad was no more than a nominal Christian virtually to the end of his life, he agreed with mother that we children should have a firm grounding in the church, wherever we happened to be living at the moment.

At the time of my surprising conception the family was living on a farm near Lindsborg, Kansas, in what are politely called "straitened circumstances." There was always enough to eat, but the financial burdens were great; it was a kind of near-poverty. Rudy, by then full-grown, revered his parents but had no illusions about their economic status. One day when mother's pregnancy became obvious, the seriousness of the situation struck him forcibly, and he couldn't hide his disapproval. "Mom, what in the world?" he burst out. "You already have your family. What's the big idea?" There was nothing she could say. What was done was done.

Once I entered this world, however, I was never treated like an unwanted child. There was more than enough love to go around. My sisters and brothers as well as my patient mother filled my childhood with affection and attention.

My only real memories of dad are fleeting ones, for he died when I was four years old. And my need to know him — or at least know about him — came much later when I tried to piece together a picture of dad from the recollections of others in the family.

Throughout his restless years, dad must have been tormented by unrealizable goals while driven to provide for a big family. Mother was the anchor: steady, resourceful, calm, and full of faith. Rudy was conscientious and serious-minded, and my sisters were rather like him in this. Bill and Bob, by contrast, could have served as models for Tom Sawyer and Huckleberry Finn at their most obstreperous.

There were grim times and good times. Both dad and mother loved music, and our home was full of it. Dad was a competent amateur musician, mother played the organ and piano, Aunt Jenny the guitar, and Uncle Oscar the mandolin. At family reunions there were sure to be several stringed instruments and an accordion, and the singing was something to hear. One by one my brothers and sisters fell into the family pattern. Rudy, a violinist, and Marie, a pianist, were especially accomplished. Bob and Bill played guitars, and Ken later followed in their footsteps.

Whatever the year may have held in the way of crises and drudgery, at Christmas time strong Swedish-American traditions were invoked to create an atmosphere of celebration: Julotta, the pre-dawn worship service; gifts for everyone; and a feast of potato sausage, lingonberries, and lutefisk.

Dad's farming was hardly worthy of the name. He kept busy with building projects, which interested him and put shoes on the children's feet, while farm chores were left to my older brothers and my mother. The uncles who lived on adjoining property were helpful and cooperative, sharing their heavy equipment and advice. At length even dad's pretense at farming was dropped, when he announced, a few months after my birth, that he had found a new career, that was sure to improve their situation.

A post office contract was up for bids in Salina, Kansas: a four-year contract to haul mail from the post office to the Union Station. To dad it was El Dorado. Rudy, who at twenty had a firmer grasp on reality, raised loud protests, but my father was adamant. He bid on the job and was awarded the contract.

No wonder! His bid was so low that there was no possibility of making money on the job. Worse, dad used the proceeds from the sale of the farm to buy three trucks.

Soon my father was back at his carpentry work, which meant that the burden of the mail contract fell on Rudy and Bill. (Bob then had a steady job at a meat-packing house.) Dad had not taken into consideration that Salina was a central point where the government sent all sorts of federal papers for storage. These papers came in carload lots, and there was no way to handle the great bulk of mail without hiring the Salina Transfer Company and its big trucks. With that went any hope of profit. What remained was the need to break even and fulfill the terms of the contract.

For Rudy — and, to a lesser extent, for Bill — it was a grind. Rudy's schedule was fiendish. He would get up early in the morning to go to a harmony class at Bethany College, then further classes throughout the day, then the night shift at the post office where he spent hours practicing the violin between trains. At three o'clock in the morning he met the last train, then went home for two hours of sleep before starting the whole routine again.

That exhausting regimen might have crushed a young man's spirit, but Rudy has a great emotional salve in music. It was his passion, almost his life's blood.

Partly because of the presence of Bethany College, nearby Lindsborg had become a midwestern cultural center, with an annual festival of music and art. Great stars of the Metropolitan Opera often performed, such as Ernestine Schumann-Heink. Rudy sang in the chorus and played in the orchestra at Bethany, and one of my earliest musical memories is a magnificent performance of Handel's *Messiah* there under the baton of the revered Professor Brase. The influence of Lindsborg spilled over into nearby Salina, and there was always music. And my family was always a part of it.

The post office contract finally ran out. Dad's life was running out, too, but we didn't know it. If anyone suspected, it was dad himself, for that year he took out an insurance policy on his life. His gregariousness and affability, plus the fact that he was an incredibly hard worker, may have concealed from his family and friends the fact that his health was far from robust.

Dad had made his last move, from Salina to Topeka, following the mail truck ordeal, when it suddenly became obvious that he was seriously ill.

Mother's heart must have ached when she saw the man she loved crumbling before her eyes, but if he was indeed dying there was something of far greater importance than brooding about her impending loss. She knew as well as dad himself that his relationship with God had never gone beyond conventional church-going. How could she bear to see him slip away without having made a conscious decision to trust the Lord, appropriate the salvation He had secured, and know the joy of a personal relationship with Him?

In her agitation mother did not trust herself to challenge dad with this matter of eternal urgency. But she did the best she could by calling her pastor who came and spent most of the night with my father. During those hours dad came to grips with his sinful condition and cast himself on the mercy of God. The following morning he gave testimony to his faith in Christ and died peacefully. He was forty-five years old.

* * *

The death of my father may have left a permanent scar on my four-year-old psyche — most psychologists would insist on the unavoidability of this, and I would not argue the point — but on a conscious level I did not suffer greatly. His death changed forever the pattern of our family life, but my mother and brothers and sisters must have tried hard to shield me from adverse affects. The loss of dad was much more painful for Kenny who was then ten years old, an age when boys acutely need the companionship and example of a father.

Marie and Mabel helped mother in every way they could. Rudy — by then immersed in the musical life of the area as a conductor and teacher — was always to be depended upon;

young Ken willingly took up his share of the burden; and even Bob and Bill — "the Katzenjammer Kids" — contributed to the family solidarity. On the surface these two had a recklessness and irresponsibility which none of the other Petersons showed. Nevertheless they were fundamentally decent youngsters and were never lazy.

Just before his death, dad had been earning a respectable living as a carpenter, and he had set us up in a comfortable rented house. Thanks to his insurance policy, we continued to live in pleasant circumstances for a time, but eventually the money ran out and with it went the house. We were reduced to living in what was not much more than a hovel.

Confronted with the necessity of providing for her younger children, and having spent her entire adult life as a wife and mother without the thought of an outside "career," mother did what she could: housework.

No one told me we were hovering on the edge of poverty, and I had one of the happiest childhoods imaginable. Though we had little in a material sense, our home was full of fun and joy, more than enough to go around. Even the material portion could be stretched to accommodate "one more." When Bob married young and his wife died in childbirth, the baby, Donald Ray, was figuratively adopted by my mother. Only a few years younger than I, he was more like a brother to me than a nephew, and even when Bob later remarried Donald continued to live with us much of the time.

From the vantage-point of half a century I don't doubt that the Lord always had us in the palm of His hand. There were Grandfather Nelson's prayers, and Grandmother Peterson's, and mother's, and the church family of which we were very much a part.

The Covenant Church in Salina came to our rescue with an old parsonage where we could live in exchange for doing janitorial work. Our living standard improved considerably, though the house was drafty and showing its age.

Rudy, Bob, Bill, and Mabel were now on their own, but

Marie, Ken, and I still lived at home. Mother often left home early for some housecleaning job, so Ken and I usually grabbed a quick breakfast by ourselves before going off to school. In the evening the family was together, with Marie or my mother preparing supper.

Saturdays were devoted to cleaning the old Mission Church. My job was to dust every bench before I could go out to play, and soon I had it down to a science. Ken's responsibility was greater, and mother, too, did her part. She also played the piano for some of the church functions. Mother was a hard and tireless worker, calm and resourceful as a parent.

And we nearly lost her.

The ancient coal furnace in the parsonage had been converted into one using city gas, more efficient but creating its own problems. Because we were always on the brink of financial ruin, mother used the gas furnace parsimoniously. In summer it was never used, of course, and in winter it was turned off at night. We alternately shivered and smothered under mountains of quilts.

A gentleman from the gas company called from time to time to suggest, ever so tactfully, that if we could pay just a bit on the gas bill — three months in arrears — they wouldn't have to cut off our supply. Somehow the bill was always paid and the gas stayed on. Small wonder mother doled it out like the precious commodity it was; small wonder our teeth chattered through frigid winter nights!

One morning mother went down to the basement to light the furnace, not knowing there was an accumulation of gas which had leaked. When she struck a match, an explosion shook the house. We came running to find mother in her nightgown, moaning and struggling up the basement stairs in a state of shock. Her eyebrows and some of her hair were gone; charred flesh hung from her arms.

A workman rushed in from the electric company next door and applied first aid. Then mother was taken to the hospital where she remained for weeks. Eventually her recovery was complete except for some scarring on her arms — but it was a close call.

This near tragedy scared the wits out of me, and paradoxically it brought me one unexpected benefit.

My sixth grade teacher, Miss Stewart, had been presented with a nearly new pair of boy's boots to be given away. Another student and I, both of us from needy families, were summoned to her office. The boots would go to whichever one of us they fit better. As it happened, they fit us both perfectly, and my spirits sank. Oh, how I wanted those wonderful boots!

Miss Stewart considered for a moment and then said, "Well, I think we're going to let John have them because his mother is in the hospital."

I wore the boots happily all through the sixth grade, yet there was something bitter about the experience. I finally realized how poor we were. One of my best pals was one of the town's "rich boys," and I became acutely aware of the economic contrast between his family's condition and mine. Though I never went hungry and though there was tremendous security in the love my family showed for one another, the situation made for some embarrassment and moments of real anxiety.

For example, there was no money for a school "activitics card." Nor could my mother afford to buy my textbooks. By the time I entered ninth grade, I had learned to dread the moment when the "poor kids" would be summoned from their classrooms to the school office to pick up books provided through public funds. Didn't anyone in the school administration realize how cruel this practice was to youngsters: to hear our names announced loudly as charity cases, to have to parade our poverty before our fellow students?

My homeroom teacher, Mr. Brooks, must have sensed my suffering, for he fabricated some errand and sent me to the office five minutes before that terrible roll was called. What made him single me out for this kindness I do not know. Perhaps he was one of those teachers with a keen sensitivity to the psychological makeup of his students, aware that the situation was more painful to some than to others.

My family, of course, was not alone. The Great Depression was upon us, and poverty — both abject and "genteel" — was all around. Twice a week I used to walk several miles to get free milk, doled out by the county authorities. The onus of "welfare" was in those days, I think, far heavier than it is today, especially to people schooled in the discipline of hard work, independence, and rugged individualism.

Between the income from mother's housework chores and the church job which paid our rent, we scraped by, although sometimes it seemed that even nature was involved in a conspiracy to make life more difficult. With the economic depression came the dust storms that swept the Midwest in the early thirties. Our Saturday duty, the cleaning of the church, became more exasperating with a thick film of prairie dust over all. I knew each elusive nook and cranny of those rounded church pews.

But I loved that church, despite the cleaning chores. The music was thrilling — great congregational singing, accompanied by a pump organ and a piano, at which my sister Marie presided — and there were warmhearted (if seemingly longwinded) sermons by preachers in swallowtail coats. One of the pastors who meant much to me was Gilbert Otteson, who came to our town after having been in evangelistic work, primarily as a song leader. He was a fine singer himself and a marvelous preacher. I attended his confirmation class where the gospel was presented with fervor. Although at the time I didn't receive Christ in a personal way, all these experiences were laying a groundwork for the future. In the Sunday school, too, I was learning much Scripture. Later, when I came to the point of yielding my life to Christ, I would realize what a solid foundation had been laid in the Covenant congregation.

My first regular church choir experience was there under my brother Rudy's direction, and often we visited other churches in the area to present concerts. When Rudy chose the cantata "Olivet to Calvary," I did one of the tenor solos as a boy soprano. We even traveled to Topeka to repeat the performance.

Marie had taken me under her wing, and although she never taught me piano (which I regret to this day), she coached my singing. We performed all over the city, for clubs, church groups and lodges, and in recitals.

Marie had a remarkable talent and had studied piano for years, despite the lack of money for lessons. After all these decades I have discovered that it was Rudy who managed it, paying her tuition at the conservatory. Then the best teacher in town, a Professor Wagstaff, took an interest in my sister and offered to give her free lessons. He had a studio in his home, which I passed on my way from school, and I would see him — a distinguished-looking man in a wing collar — standing on the porch, beating time with his cane while his students labored at the keyboard inside the house. Professor Wagstaff was a distinguished teacher and a distinct character, playing the role of the musical pedagogue to the hilt.

Though Marie had no salary at the church, there was always a gift of money from the congregation at Christmas time. She made sure that each of us got a share, and for years that "made" our Christmas. It was one of the added blessings by which the Lord took care of us.

Summers were paradise for a spindly town kid like me. During the school year I did my best to keep up with the usual games boys played — sandlot baseball and the like — but when the school year ended I headed for the farm, and there, under the care of Uncle Harry and Aunt Jenny, I blossomed.

Uncle Harry, who was married to my mother's sister, was like a big kid himself. He was forever going fishing or puttering about. How he got his crops planted and harvested was a mystery, for he never seemed to be on any kind of conventional schedule. Childless, he became a surrogate father to me, and I loved him. His hearty, vulgar conversation raised eyebrows among grownups in the family, but we children — my cousins from adjoining farms and I — thought he was great.

Ostensibly I was to help out on the farm, and I *did* help where I could, hoeing cockleburrs out of the corn and milking one gentle cow which was my personal responsibility. Actually, however, my summers consisted of running in the sunshine, stocking up on marvelous home-cooked farm fare, playing with my cousins, riding horseback, and tagging along after Uncle Harry.

On hot nights he joined me on the front porch of the farmhouse where I slept, always reminding me to make sure the screen door was shut tight. "We don't want any rattlers in the house, John." He wasn't kidding. There *were* rattlesnakes in the pastures and fields, and they would often find their way to the area of the farm buildings. At harvest time when the threshing crew came around — a tremendous event in my young life — invariably a sleepy rattler would be roused from under one of the grain shocks.

Saturday afternoon brought a ritual adventure, a trip to nearby Lost Springs or to Lincolnville a few miles further along the road, the Model A piled high with eggs and produce for market. Visiting the tonsorial parlor was a special treat because the genial German barber had taken a shine to me and could always be counted on to give me a nickel for an ice cream cone or a Baby Ruth candy bar.

At summer's end I would be tanned, toughened, and more than ready to go home to Salina to my family.

Salina was a provincial, sleepy midwestern town of just over twenty thousand. Not strictly a farm town, for there was some industry. Though nothing really dramatic ever happened there, Salina was a metropolis to me, and after a placid summer on Uncle Harry's farm town life was even more of a bustle.

My routine centered around the family, the public school, and the Covenant Church, which provided a secure spiritual home. Like my brother Ken, I had such a natural bent for sacred things that many of the church folk assumed we would both one day be preachers. In Sunday School we toiled through the main history of the Bible, almost by osmosis packing away a lot of information. Our teachers were laymen, but well grounded in the Scriptures. If we looked back now on their teaching methods, I suppose we would find them strict and old-fashioned. Nevertheless, we learned — and plenty.

I kindled to anything and everything musical in the church. That setting provided food for the two strong elements in my nature: the love of music, which must have come primarily from the Peterson side of the family, and the piety, with which I associate my mother and the Nelsons.

From infancy I had been exposed to a broad spectrum of music. We may have been poor, but the Petersons — largely through their musical talents — were actively involved in the cultural life of the city, and I was immensely proud of them. Rudy and Marie were serious musicians, surrounding us with the sounds of Bach, Beethoven, and the lighter classics. Bill had taken up the trombone as a teen-ager, and he became an excellent player — versatile, too: he, Bob, and later Kenny were all guitarists of professional quality.

At church there was a wide range of sacred music, from hymns and gospel songs to cantatas and oratorios. School provided operettas, concerts, glee clubs, bands, and the like, while the radio supplied me with another insight into the world of music. For a time I was captivated by the sound of the big bands and would sit glued to the radio for hours on end under the spell of such popular idols as Glenn Miller, Henry Busse, and Eddy Duchin.

Impressed by the accomplishments of my family, I experimented with both piano and guitar until I could produce something approximating music. But I was primarily interested in singing, for God had gifted me with a naturally good voice — strong, clear, sweet, and well-focused. One of my schoolteachers, Paul Thornton, arranged for me to hear and see touring musical productions, including the opera company from Chicago. My job was to hand out programs; my reward, free entree to the performance. Thus I heard *Il Trovatore*, *Faust*, and other great works. It all fed my desire to become a professional singer. I even dreamed of becoming an opera star!

The Covenant Church itself did not lack concert music — I remember a recital Rudy presented in the church with a string quartet from the conservatory. The prevailing attitude toward the legitimate theater and movies, however, was another thing. These were considered to be of the devil. Opera, okay — perhaps because the sheer grandeur of the music overwhelmed the often gory, melodramatic, sex-drenched librettos. The concert hall, too, was fine. But not the theater!

Other deadly sins were dancing, card-playing, and gambling. It is amusing to recall, however, that our church had no particular stricture against the use of tobacco. Alcohol was anathema, but a lot of churchmen chewed tobacco or snuff. Tobacco was considered "one of God's blessed herbs"!

Wrapped up in music and the life of the church, I never strayed into real trouble, as some of my contemporaries did, but I had mischievous moments. One summer during Daily Vacation Bible School I pulled a trick that put me in the doghouse for about a week.

Every morning the DVBS teachers met for prayer in a basement room of the church. Just before the Fourth of July I happened to get my hands on one of those firecrackers known as two-inch busters. I took it down into the basement, lit it, and shoved it under the door while the teachers were praying. The size of the explosion in that resonant basement room was satisfying beyond my wildest dreams.

Never doubting that I would be found out, I got a board and put it in the seat of my trousers, and when I walked down the aisle of the church to take my place in the front row the hundred or more kids in the room roared with laughter. I was, of course, expelled from DVBS for the rest of the session. My mother was embarrassed, and this made my mortification almost unbearable. But the teachers took pity on me and allowed me to return for the final program when awards were given out. Though I had missed a week of school, I won some awards just the same, and my being allowed to receive them was the sign that my boyish escapade had been forgiven.

My first attempts at writing did not involve songs at all, but poetry. For several years during high school I thought seriously about becoming a poet. I read verse day after day, far beyond what my classes required, and then I would try to write. I never had enough self-confidence to try to get my verses published, but those attempts at poetry were good preparation for writing song lyrics.

The themes I chose were often from nature, history, fantasy, and bits of local color. Much of my poetry, however, was in a spiritual vein:

I'll follow Thee, I'll follow Thee
Through waters dark and deep;
I'll follow Thee o'er deserts dry,
And over rocky steep.
I'll bravely stand amid the flames
Of a fiery furnace bright;
I'll joy in trials great or small –
In any other plight.
I'll suffer shame and sad remorse,
I'll suffer utter loss.
I'll don the robes of grief and pain
And carry any cross

*   *   *   *

If only it will draw me close,
And closer, Lord, to Thee;
If only it will bring Thee near,
And nearer, Lord, to me.

Juvenile? Of course. Simple and predictable. But the sentiments were heartfelt.

5

Boca Raton . . . 1975

We're into the preliminary part of the concert now. Beverly Terrell's rich soprano fills the auditorium: "The Lord is my light and my salvation; whom then shall I fear? Whom then shall I fear?"

Behind her the choir members listen enthralled. I'm listening, too, but my mind keeps racing, and I find the events of the past week tumbling about in a kaleidoscope of sounds and images.

What a week! A blaze of activity, learning, laughter, and fellowship with old friends and the joy of discovering new ones. Heart-stopping moments, too, like when the stranger came up to me and said that he, after years of churchgoing and "decent living," had finally found Christ in a personal way while singing in a performance of one of my cantatas. Can one begin to measure the gratitude a composer feels to hear a testimony like that?

Yes, it has been a week to remember. Choir directors and singers have come from all over the country, taking valuable time from their schedules and paying significant sums of money for travel and expenses and tuition to learn from me and my fellow faculty members in this National Church Music Leadership Conference.

Beyond that, they've learned this new piece of music. The rehearsal schedule alone was taxing, even had there been no other activities and classes. They've looked to me for advice and expertise, and I've given my best. But I wonder what they would think if I took them into a dusty corner of the past and told them about my first big failure as a choir director. . . .

It was more than a golden opportunity. To me it looked like pure platinum. At the time, I had completed my formal education and was on the staff of Moody Bible Institute's radio station, struggling on a salary of $250 a month with a wife and three children to support. Out of nowhere came a job offer as director of choral music for one of Chicago's fine churches. I didn't know much about choral music, but this offer had to be of God. It was His way of easing the burden — doubling my income.

But I was in way over my head. There was no way I could handle that job! Even now I can recall the sinking feeling of knowing I was not ready. Everyone sympathized; everyone tried to make the best of it. But the fact remained: I was a big, resounding failure. I finally shuffled away, sadder, wiser, and very much humbled by the extent of my limitations.

I still believe God was in it, for I know He doesn't make mistakes. He had something to teach me that I could not have learned in any other way. From the time I gave myself heart and soul to the Lord, nothing has happened to me — good or bad in the world's eyes, disappointing or exhilarating — that fails to fit into the mosaic of His master plan. I would believe this even if He stripped me of worldly goods and honors and left me on a trash heap covered with boils. The Lord is faithful; the Lord is trustworthy.

Listen, you men and women up there in the choir – listen, everyone: Whatever you have in the way of a talent, large or small, put it in God's hands. You may feel inadequate, as I have often felt. Never mind. All He needs is a yielded instrument – that's the key to everything. When we make ourselves available to God, He will use us. Not because our talent is great, but because it is in His hands.

My deepest regrets in life are not jobs at which I failed, nor human relationships in which I did not give my best, but rather — Why haven't I prayed more? Loved God more? Carried a greater burden for His work and His people and a lost world?

My most satisfying moments have been in His presence. Human achievements, no matter how spectacular, without God's touch will not stand the test of judgment. When we face the fiery test of His judgment, they will be but "wood, hay, and stubble."

Disappointments are hard to take. My experience in the Chicago church was a fiasco, and there were other disappointments along the way. But I did not brood about them, and the Lord never let me grow bitter either. Trusting that He was in overall control, I "buried" the Chicago episode and eventually went on to a choir I *was* able to handle, developing through hard work and experience, often getting more from the people who sang under my direction than they ever got from me.

Little by little my confidence increased, until at last I had the assurance that this was a calling I could grow into, and it happened. In a few moments I'll face a great choir, a professional orchestra, and a multitude of listeners. I can be grateful for the failures as well as for the triumphs, for without all those experiences I would not be here tonight.

The first part of the program is over, and the congregation is singing "God Bless America." Amen.

6

A peculiar kind of insecurity dogged me throughout my childhood. I can't account for it, and I can't deny it. Today I recognize my vain idiosyncrasies and perfectionist fetish for what they are, even as I repeatedly try to conquer them. I know also that their origins lie deep in the fears and feelings of inadequacy I conjured up as a youngster.

I always had good health, yet fancied that I was frail, sickly. From time to time I would convince myself that I was fated to die young without realizing any of my potential, and this would fill me with melancholy. There was no evidence of invalidism, but the fantasy persisted.

Sure, I was thin — painfully thin — and as a result often shy and easily insulted. Good natured references to my rail-like physique were magnified into cruel digs. And because I knew on a conscious level that these remarks were not intended to hurt me, I had to laugh along with the joke and absorb the hurt deep in my soul. Even when I reached manhood a sally about my appearance still cut deep. I was getting ready for induction into the army when one of my brothers — perhaps trying to cheer me up — said, "They'll never be able to shoot you, John, if you remember to turn sideways." I gritted my teeth, grinned, and the conversation changed course, but it was as if a sharp knife had dug into a mass of old scar tissue.

I would not, however, leave the impression of a tortured, tormented youth. Quite the contrary. I was loved, often pampered, my life full of satisfactions. My fears and dark fantasies were intermittent, yet strong enough to make a permanent impression on my emotions. I live with them to this day.

Happily, early in childhood I found a place of power which brought me attention and admiration. My God-given singing voice provided me with countless opportunities to excel. For some years I concentrated on this "place in the sun" to an almost obsessive degree.

My sister Marie coached my singing and instilled in me the conviction that anything less than the best I was capable of was unacceptable. Far from being a chore, getting up before an audience gave me ego rewards I might not have gotten elsewhere. With Marie beside me at the piano, and with the knowledge that we were well-prepared and adequate to the occasion, I got tremendous satisfaction from the experience, no matter how insecure I might be in other respects. It also inflated my grandiose dreams for the future. How easy it was to envision myself on the stage of a concert hall or opera house while thousands of people sat on the edges of their seats to catch the golden tones pouring forth from my throat!

Not that I *always* felt adequate to perform. At times I was overtaken by anxiety (I couldn't possibly do this thing!) and almost had to be pushed onto the stage. Once I was up there, however, I settled down and did pretty well.

One such occasion was when talent scouts for the Original Amateur Hour came to town and Marie insisted I try out for the show. Anyone of my generation who owned a radio back in the thirties and forties will remember Major Edward Bowes, a tremendously popular broadcaster of the period — almost an

American institution. Each week he masterminded a nationwide radio broadcast. He also had troupes traveling back and forth across the land, performing in theaters and school auditoriums and looking for fresh talent.

Irish tenors, marimba players, impressionists, tap dancers, bell-ringers — you name it: Major Bowes would find some way to use it. On his show were people who made "music" by cracking their knuckles and expelling air from balloons. Did you play the bones, the kazoo, the harmonica, the comb? If you trotted down to the armory and did your act for his talent scouts, who knows? You might win a short-term contract with the troupe and get to see some of the country.

With my sister pushing and coaxing, I went to the audition. But when I saw that roomful of hopeful would-be vaudevillians, I froze. Sure, they were just Salina folks like me, but I was intimidated. I waited until everyone else had a turn before I would get up and sing, and no one was more surprised than I when I won the contest.

As a result of the Major Bowes episode, I got some free vocal lessons from an outstanding local teacher, plus another surprising chance to stand in the spotlight. The manager of Salina's radio station KFBI suggested I try a fifteen-minute broadcast, singing old folk songs with an organ accompaniment. He had even lined up the Electrolux dealer as a sponsor for the show and could pay me something — incredible! My "professional career" lasted only a few months, but my brief fame as "The Singing Farm Boy" seemed tremendously significant to me. It also enabled me to earn some money, which helped out with the family finances. That was important in depression days.

It was natural for a youngster to magnify these moments of triumph and invest them with an importance they didn't deserve. The more so when one considers what kind of boy I was: often assailed with a sense of inferiority and gloomy forebodings of a premature death. I've always had wide swings of mood, from depression to elation, and these were exaggerated by the confusing natural forces of adolescence at work in my body.

All of this, however, receded to insignificance when compared to the dramatic spiritual changes taking place in my family — changes which revolutionized my attitude and, more than anything else, shaped my destiny.

A complete turnaround in the life of my brother Bill signaled this revolution. In time it touched us all, transforming our relationship as a family and changing each of us as individuals.

While my father was still living and Bill and Bob were in their teens, they were such hellions that it was a kind of miracle they never got into serious trouble with the law. Not being able to buy whiskey in Salina, they regularly made trips to Kansas City to replenish their stock of bootleg hooch — trips which the Salina County sheriff took a great interest in, as he was morally certain of the motivation behind them. Fortunately or unfortunately, my brothers had a chum in the police department who warned them when they were going to be tailed.

One night after such a warning they were out joy-riding with their girl friends in Bill's Paige Eight, and they led the patrol car a merry chase over hills and rough roads for several hours. Finally tiring of the game, they pulled up at a dance hall with the police right behind them. My brothers and the car were thoroughly frisked, but they were "clean."

On another occasion they were less fortunate. After an evening of dancing at the Linger Longer, Bob and Bill and their dates were approached by two men who identified themselves as sheriff's deputies. Bob challenged them to show their credentials, and when they refused, the battle was on.

It was quite a brawl, with some onlookers coming to my brothers' assistance and others siding with the deputies. Bob was hit on the head with a blackjack, and after the fight subsided he and Bill were hauled off to spend the night in the county jail. They considered this very unjust, for neither of them was drunk (that time!). The next morning the judge found them guilty of disturbing the peace and ordered them to pay a fine of thirty-five dollars. Their friends came to the rescue with the required amount in small coins. Vastly irritated, the judge finally counted out the dimes and nickles and let Bob and Bill go.

Dad's death sobered them temporarily, but before long they were back flirting with disaster. They both managed to stay employed most of the time, however. When Bill found work as a printer's devil for the *Salina Journal,* he declared that the job description fit him to a tee.

Actually, from the vantage point of 1975, the deviltry of my brothers in the twenties does not look so appalling. The passage of time and our awareness of today's vices and aberrations put a pale tone — almost a quaintness — on their youthful rebelliousness. But consider how it must have seemed to my mother and her contemporaries — pious, conservative folk whose ethics and morals grew out of a pioneer heritage reinforced by the strictures of the Covenant Church. Boozing, gambling, fast driving, and sheriff-baiting were no jokes to them, but matters of awful consequence. Which is, no doubt, why such practices were irresistible to "the Katzenjammer Kids" and their cronies, swinging along in the heady, "emancipated" tempo of the roaring twenties.

It all might have ended tragically but for something of eternal significance that took place in the community.

In the city of Salina there was a group of businessmen — some of them from the Covenant Church — among whom God began to move in a special way. One by one these men yielded themselves to the Lord. Partly, I suppose because of their prominence as business people, this made quite an impact on the community.

Among this group were two men I remember in particular: Julius Brandt and Ed Fehr. They and others were witnessing to their newfound faith in a powerful, persuasive way. Ed Fehr became the leader of a Bible class, and he proved to be a gifted teacher. More and more people were drawn into the circle as they saw the living Lord at work.

From the Bible class emerged an independent church called the Salina Bible Hall whose ranks were swelled by new converts and people attracted from other churches in the city — including our own Covenant Church. Of course there was suspicion and resentment among some Christians in the established churches, but the work prospered.

All this was known to our family. Clearly something extraordinary was happening among Brandt and Fehr and the many others who clustered about them.

One night when he was pretty drunk, my brother Bill went speeding down Ninth Street in Salina, paying no attention to traffic lights or anything else. He breezed through fifteen intersections without mishap, and the next morning when he woke up he realized what he had done and how lucky he was to have escaped alive — and without killing or maiming anyone else. He was so shaken that the thought came: *Was it only luck, or was the Lord watching over me?*

No matter how hard he tried to put this thought out of his mind, it kept coming back to haunt him.

At that time Bill was playing trombone in the local symphony orchestra and hoping for a job with a prominent dance band. A few days after the drunk-driving incident, he went to Kansas City to audition for a nationally known orchestra leader, who promptly offered him a job. For some reason Bill declined to sign a contract immediately, but promised to return the following week to do so.

He came home to Salina troubled, unaware that the Holy Spirit was working in his heart. One evening mother found him sitting in an overstuffed chair next to an end table on which lay a Bible. He looked so strange that she said, "Bill, are you all right?" He didn't answer, and she left him to his thoughts.

Suddenly he picked up the Bible and it fell open to Matthew 11:28 — "Come unto me all ye that labor and are heavy laden and I will give you rest." Just as suddenly, Bill felt a strong urge to telephone Julius Brandt, one man who seemed to be living truly as a Christian. Obeying this impulse, he called

Mr. Brandt, who told Bill he was scheduled to speak at a banquet that evening but would be happy to see him the following night.

My brother hung up the phone, pulled himself together, and left the house to attend an orchestra rehearsal, only to discover that the rehearsal had been rescheduled. Once more there was that strong impulse to telephone Julius Brandt, and once more Bill obeyed it. As soon as Brandt picked up the phone, he said, "Bill, come on over. The banquet has been postponed."

Feeling foolish and a bit ashamed — what if his friends could see him now? — Bill went to Brandt's house and was warmly received. After some small talk, the older man got to the point: "Bill, what did you want to see me about? I'm sure you didn't come just to pay a social call."

A war was being fought in my brother's soul — Satan fighting to retain his own — but at last Bill said that if there was a God, he wanted to find Him.

Julius Brandt opened up the Word of God and showed Bill how he could receive Christ. They got down on their knees together, and my brother haltingly asked God to accept him as His child and to forgive all his sins.

"Suddenly," Bill says, "a heavy burden rolled off my heart and a great peace and joy flooded my soul."

He went home, took mother in his arms, kissed her for the first time in his adult life, and said, "Mother, I have found your Christ as my Savior."

His transformation was immediate and amazingly complete. The very next day Bill found his vocabulary changed, and when his boss remarked on the lack of cuss words, my brother told him what had happened. The following weekend he returned, as promised, to Kansas City, where he told the bandleader that he could not sign the contract because he had found a new friend — Jesus.

Talk about radical conversions! In a moment Bill was changed from a wild, carousing young man to a committed

Christian. He started to pray and read the Bible, and though — he said — he couldn't understand it at first, he could believe it.

Bill's conversion also had a sensational effect on our family. Even as a child I knew that something extraordinary had taken place. Bill's whole life was rearranged. He had been active in a dance band which met in our home to rehearse; after he came to Christ, the rehearsals became prayer meetings.

His drinking pals scoffed, but Bill simply gave them his testimony. He was short on knowledge of the Word, but he had had an experience with Christ and to this he bore witness. Some called him a fanatic, and he didn't mind. He knew he was a child of God, and he wanted the whole world to know about his Lord and Savior.

Kenny was coming home from the movies one night when Bill collared him and spoke to him about Jesus. "I do want Him," Ken said. Then and there he made his decision, accepted Christ as his Lord, and began a lifelong commitment.

But our brother Bob was the heaviest burden on Bill's heart, for he insisted that all he wanted was the life he had. At one point he became so enraged at Bill's witnessing to him that he threatened to give Bill the beating of his life if he didn't "get the hell out" and leave him alone. Bob was married now, but this change in his status had not altered his wayward life style.

Realizing that continuing in this vein was fruitless, Bill got together with V. E. Peterson (no relation), another recent convert, to pray about the matter. They spent many hours in a car in front of Bob's house, entreating the Lord to melt his heart.

Soon a whole group of people from the Salina Bible Hall were praying for Bob, and their prayers were answered. Not long afterward, both Bob and his wife yielded their lives to Christ. The transformation in Bob was no less striking than that in Bill. He was a totally new person, on fire for the Lord.

He would go out on his bicycle, carrying his guitar, and when he saw a group of men working he would stop and say,

"Fellows, can I sing you a song?" Then he would sing a gospel song and give his testimony.

Ken, too, was riding on the whirlwind of the Spirit. Though still only a boy, he became a Sunday school teacher and a preacher, with such an intense zeal that I came to look on him as little short of divine!

Rudy, however, was somewhat aloof. Married, with his own home, he was a bit insulated from the work of God that was so influential in our family. As a young man in the Covenant church he had made a profession of faith, and he was circumspect and conscientious, but not until some years later, after he had moved to Seattle, did he enter wholly into the new life. When he did, it was real and lasting.

The Salina Bible Hall continued to enjoy the blessing of God, but Ed Fehr, who had shepherded the group for so many months, gave up the leadership and a new pastor, Nye J. Langmade, was called. Pastor Langmade gave the work new impetus and began a ministry that was to have an impact on the entire state of Kansas. He became a leader in the independent church movement, serving for a time as president of the Independent Fundamental Churches of America. It was through his ministry that my sister Mabel came to know the Lord. And so the work of God which began with those few dedicated businessmen continued to grow.

I was not a part of it because mother, Marie, Ken, and I were still involved in the Covenant church, where Marie had made her decision for Christ during an evangelistic service some time earlier. We would attend services at the Salina Bible Hall, however, for Bob, Bill, and Mabel were in it heart and soul.

The preaching was powerful. I was at the church one night with a group of friends — it was the first time I had found courage to sit by one of the girls and we had planned to go out afterward for a Coke — when, despite my excitement over the prospect of my first "date," I found myself caught up in the sermon. Mr. Langmade was preaching on a text from Daniel:

"Thou art weighed in the balances and found wanting."

As the sermon progressed, a struggle began to take place in my heart. It was as if I were alone, faced with the demands of a stern and righteous God, confronted by the issues of sin and judgment so clearly that there was no room for evasion — no place to hide. What had happened in my family and in the community had made a strong impression on me, but now, for the first time, I was touched in a personal way.

True, I was a "good boy," with an affinity for spiritual things. But that was not the issue. Along with every other human being, I was weighed in the balances and found wanting, for I had not personally appropriated the work of Christ, and I knew it. God's grace and love were there in abundance — I knew a lot about them. But the overwhelming reality of God's righteous judgment! There it was: terrible, holy, inevitable, and it applied to me, John Peterson. I had not gone God's way. I felt the irresistible pull of the gospel as the only sufficient way out of my burden of guilt.

The sermon ended, and the invitation was given to step forward and make a decision for Christ. I came back to earth, turned to my cousin beside me and the two girls who were with us and said, "Any of you want to go forward?" They all shook their heads.

This made my inner battle more painful, for I knew I would have to walk that aisle alone. How could I make myself so vulnerable in the eyes of my companions and the other people in the church? But I must . . . I must.

Somehow I did it, and when I reached the front of the church I found my brother Ken kneeling beside me with an open Bible. Together we read the familiar verses dealing with Christ's sacrifice and the salvation which only He could provide. Suddenly they came into sharp, individual focus. Those verses had my name on them. Ken and I prayed together, my resistance melted, and I gave my heart to Christ.

* * *

My decision brought an immediate sense of relief. Now I could count myself on God's side, like the other members of my family. If my school chums failed to grasp the fact that something of importance had happened to me, that was a matter of no great consequence. I knew where I stood, and if I was too reticent to speak of my decision openly, it did not trouble me.

But as the months passed, the flame of my conversion began to flicker fitfully. My thirteenth birthday came and went. I was in limbo: no longer a child, not yet an adult, struggling with the usual confusing problems of adolescence. So I was a Christian! What did it *mean* in terms of my day-to-day life — my schoolwork, my friends, my dreams of a singing career? The Lord held me close, but I could not avoid nagging questions about the significance of what I had experienced that night in the Salina Bible Hall. It was not that I doubted the reality of what had occurred, but perhaps, in my boyish way, I needed once more to affirm it publicly.

About a year had passed when a great Swedish evangelist named Frank Mangs came to tour the Covenant churches in America. He had already visited Chicago and now was to conduct a series of meetings in the Smokey Hill Valley in our part of the country.

Mangs preached in his native language, with Pastor Otteson beside him as a translator, but it did not diminish the impact of his message. His text was from Matthew — the passage about the man harvesting wheat, shaking out the grain, and burning the chaff. As the sermon reached its climax, I knew I would have no peace unless I went forward again and declared myself for Christ.

Basically, Mangs's message was the same as Langmade's sermon which had moved me so a year earlier. Both of them put me under strong conviction of sin. In thinking of the future and eventual judgment, I felt I wasn't ready, and it was really a fear of meeting God unprepared which brought me to a point of decision about yielding to Christ.

So once more I responded to the invitation. Once more there was prayer and a promise.

From that point on I had peace and assurance that I was a Christian. I truly believe that I had given my life to Christ the first time, but because of my youth and the fact that I was insufficiently grounded in Scripture to trust Him absolutely, the second public declaration was necessary. Shortly afterward, I was baptized.

Older Christians, seeing my need for more knowledge, encouraged me to start reading the Bible regularly. I began at Genesis and read through to the end of Revelation, ten chapters a day. All through my high school years I continued this practice until I had read through the Bible several times and developed a consistent devotional life.

7

Boca Raton . . .1975

It's an unusual audience, with a glow and glitter one doesn't often see in church. Signs of affluence and privilege everywhere: men in white coats or tailored tropical suits; hundreds of women in long dresses and mink stoles, their hair elaborately coiffured for the occasion.

The audience doesn't frighten me, however. I know people are basically the same whether they wear furs and jewelry or work shirts and blue jeans. What does intimidate me a bit tonight is a more subtle thing.

These are my people. They know me; I know them. Probably most of them have heard several of my cantatas; almost certainly they know many of my songs. A work by John Peterson is a known quantity — and what they're going to hear tonight is a distinct departure for me.

We've warned them that this new musical is different, but even so, the air of trust and expectation hanging over the audience tells me that their ears are tuned and their spirits primed for "more of the same."

This time I may have reached too far, trying to accomplish two things in one musical work: a patriotic celebration of our national heritage followed by a call to repentance and a spiritual appeal. Until tonight we have not had a chance to measure the public's response. So far the only ones who have heard the piece are people so close to the creative process, or the performance preparation, or the mechanism of business, that an unbiased reaction has been impossible.

I have to admit to some apprehension. If tonight is a disaster, I'll get over it. I've gotten over disasters before, let the Lord pick me up, and gone on to the next thing. I can do it again.

But oh, how I would hate to disappoint these people! It would be different if the audience were made up of musical sophisticates who find my work too simple, too bland, or too "square." Criticism hurts — I admit that, too — but I expect it from certain quarters.

I wouldn't be taken aback by a poor reception from people to whom both patriotism and spiritual values are passé. Nor would I be astonished to hear some gentle chiding from old friends who think I've overreached lately in the kinds of rhythms and musical effects that punctuate my more traditional sounds. Like the dear old lady who said after hearing a recent work of mine, "It's nice — but I do miss the *old* John Peterson." I know what she meant. I don't think I've gone off the deep end, but I *do* know what she meant.

No, my apprehension has to do with this audience tonight. This particular crowd under these particular circumstances.

My people. You know them — solid, respectable, salt of the earth, devout, hardworking, stable, trustworthy. Much of my life has been spent among folks like these: the farmers and small businessmen of Kansas; the teachers and preachers who spurred me on my way; the sincere and sober students and faculty members at Moody; the gospel musicians and evangelists and those who came to listen to them; the businessmen and artists with whom it was my happy experience to build a thriving concern on a small and somewhat rickety foundation.

Someone coined a term for this crowd a few years ago, a term probably born in derision: Middle America.

In the topsy-turvy world of the sixties we were suddenly made to feel uneasy because we stood for traditional values, like faith in God and love of country. Some of us never quite figured out the peculiar logic of poking fun at the very virtues that came together to form the backbone of the nation. What was there about our morality and way of life to evoke such scorn?

Most of us kept our mouths shut while strident spokesmen from right and left made us the butt of their humor and the scapegoat for their discontent.

And then, as if that wasn't bad enough, we woke up one day to discover that we had been exploited and deceived by some of the very leaders who had seemed to give voice to the things we felt but found difficult to express!

For Middle America to feel manipulated has meant shock and disillusionment. And it may be a while before we get over it.

Our values are intact, however, and I decided it was about time to underline them once again and remind us that we are still a great nation. But if that greatness is to continue, we must, as did our forefathers on many occasions, return to God in true repentance and renewed faith and commitment.

That was the genesis of tonight's new musical, *I Love America*. I'm hoping and praying it will strike a responsive chord here in the very heart of my own crowd — call it Middle America or whatever you will.

There's a timeless quality about this great audience. Yes, they look more prosperous than most of the congregations I've faced over the decades — better dressed, better fed perhaps — but the faces are the same. The needs and anticipations haven't changed, either, affluence or no affluence.

Give them a lift through these words and this music, Lord, if You will. You know I don't want to let them down.

Any more than I wanted to let them down the very first time I stood before a group of worshipers to lead the singing. . . .

Tampa, Kansas. Not in a grand auditorium or even a simple frame church, but a tent. I was a teen-ager, tagging along after my brothers. Bob, Bill, and Kenny were well known and much loved in our corner of the world as the Norse Gospel Trio. Through radio broadcasting they had reached thousands with the Good News, and they traveled throughout the Midwest and the Southwest in evangelistic meetings, singing the great old gospel songs and bringing the Word of Life through Kenny's preaching.

Bob was the song leader, but for some reason that night he pulled me out of the congregation and asked me to lead some choruses. Scared stiff, I gulped a few times and wondered what I was doing there. My big hands dangled at the ends of my long, skinny arms like a couple of hams hanging in a smokehouse. Suddenly I was all bones and not much brain. But I had to try.

I tried.

And the people were kind. They knew the songs, and despite my awkwardness and inexperience, we struggled through together. But I was sure I had been a total failure and was so embarrassed by my efforts that immediately after the service I ran out, got in the back seat of my brothers' car, and hid. No matter how much they tried to reassure me, when they had tracked me down in my hiding place, I was convinced that I hadn't done my job well and never would. A typical adolescent, I overdramatized what seemed to me to be failure, then compensated the next time by straining and struggling to do better.

8

The Norse Gospel Trio came into being not so much by design as by a happy accident. Bob and Bill had been playing guitars and singing together for years, and when Kenny approached maturity he joined them. The family enjoyed their performances without any thought that a wider audience might respond the same way. Maybe the combination was God's way of getting my brothers launched in a ministry beyond the confines of their church and circle of friends, and when the three young men had surrendered their lives to the Lord, one by one, they were ready to fall in with His plan.

There was something of a serendipity about the trio's formation. Little by little they realized that they were blending better, working together as a unit, and sounding more professional.

One day they drove to Abilene to the studios of radio station KFBI and asked for an audition. The station manager was impressed enough to arrange a time slot for them the following Sunday morning. Through the rest of the week they polished and repolished their presentation of ten gospel songs. The results were more than any of us could have anticipated, and the station made a firm offer: a Sunday morning broadcast each week. No commercial sponsor was immediately available, but KFBI would itself act as the trio's sponsor, airing the program as a public service. For a year my brothers made the trip from Salina to Abilene every Sunday without missing a broadcast. Then remote control studios were established in Salina, which was much more convenient.

The trio gained immediate popularity. Soon they had two thirty-minute programs over KFBI every weekday in addition to the Sunday broadcast. Bob, Bill, and Ken had found their avocation. They could even be called celebrities.

But radio broadcasting left something to be desired as far as a gospel ministry was concerned. My brothers wanted more: the intimate contact with their audience which could come only through personal appearances. The trio was not an end in itself, but a vehicle through which they could share the Good News which had turned them around and given them purpose and fulfillment. They began to travel throughout Kansas, Nebraska, Oklahoma, wherever they were invited, holding meeting in tents and churches for whatever length of time was available — one night stands and often extended crusades and tours.

People came from miles around to see my brothers in the flesh, to listen to their music, and to hear Ken preach, and many were won to Christ. Even today we meet people who testify that they found the Lord through the ministry of the Norse Gospel Trio a generation ago.

Sometimes they let me travel with them — a heady adventure for a boy like me. My admiration for my brothers was enormous. Their wholehearted devotion to the Lord, their music, their popularity, their showmanship, and their personalities all impressed me deeply. There were many "side benefits" of being with the trio — for instance, the fellowship with those who played host. I particularly remember some marvelous dinners among the Mennonites, who made up an enthusiastic part of the trio's audience. The Mennonites were also generous when it came to free-will offerings to keep the trio on the road.

Money was a constant problem, though lack of it never dampened our enthusiasm or brought about cancellation of services, as far as I can recall. Eventually the trio was self-supporting. My brothers *were* celebrities, in a way, for radio performers achieved a kind of star status in people's eyes, as TV personalities did later on, but the nation was in the throes of its worst economic depression and cash was hard to come by. At times one or more of my brothers worked at outside jobs to supplement their income and make the evangelistic work possible. What's more, Bill and Bob had families to support. My mother provided for me, as usual; she continued to do outside housework throughout my high school days. And in a larger sense it was the Lord who took care of us all. The trio scraped by, sometimes garnering barely enough from a free-will offering to buy a tankful of gasoline. But nobody complained about it. The work itself was the richest reward.

A high-water mark in their radio evangelistic ministry was during a period in Tulsa, Oklahoma, where they broadcast over KVOO, a clear-channel station with a huge audience. They drew mail from a half-dozen or more states.

I spent a summer with the trio in Tulsa and traveled along to many of their meetings. One which I remember vividly was held in Goaltrie, a small town in the Oklahoma panhandle. When we arrived for the service, the church was so packed that there was no way to get in through the doors. Finally the pastor led us around to the back, and we climbed through a window to get to the platform.

That resourceful pastor was not rich in worldly goods. The parsonage, as I recall, was scantily furnished and gave mute testimony to financial struggle. But my brothers and I were impressed by the man's dedication to the Lord and by his keen interest in radio broadcasting. Subsequently he found his own outstanding ministry in the medium, for the pastor's name was Theodore Epp — the same Theodore Epp who is known to millions as founder and director of the Back to the Bible broadcast ministry.

During their sojourn in Tulsa my brothers befriended a young announcer, barely twenty years old, and they got him a job with KFBI when they came back to Salina. This talented fellow sometimes traveled with the trio and was often exposed to the claims of Christ. One evening after a long conversation with Bill and the others, he said, "I would be a fool if I didn't accept Christ and what He has to offer."

Following his conversion, he sometimes helped Kenny with the preaching and proved to be as good a preacher as he was an announcer. But when he left Kansas we lost track of him. Years later, after World War II, I discovered that this man had matured to become one of the most popular newscasters in Chicago and in the whole American Broadcasting System.

Since then we have occasionally been in touch. He has written my brothers some wonderful letters and has mentioned my work several times on his national broadcasts. A few years ago he made reference to me in one of his newspaper columns, in which he gave the opinion that a lot of church music is out of tune with the younger generation. In contrast, he mentioned some of my songs with the remark, "These have a melodic, lyric quality which anybody can enjoy singing and will remember."

It was a nice tribute from an old friend, Paul Harvey.

* * *

While Bill and Bob were concerned with the music and administrative aspects of their evangelistic work, and while Ken was getting deeper and deeper into the preaching ministry, their little brother was going through the baffling metamorphosis of adolescence and trying to face up to some thorny questions about the future.

From time to time I tinkered with songwriting. My earliest

effort, the birthday song for Grandfather Nelson, had come to me one day while I sat improvising at the piano. Its warm reception surprised me but did not suggest anything of unusual importance. Later, however, when I experimented further with writing gospel songs, I was again surprised and pleased to find that I had some facility for it.

During that period it was hard for me to believe that I could do anything well, aside from singing. I did not take my writing talent seriously, and when I signed up for a course in harmony in high school, I was so insecure that I dropped out of the class almost immediately. The devil kept plaguing me with inferiority feelings, the effects of which are still with me. Time and again I've faced demands beyond my native ability and training, rarely feeling totally adequate. In each case I have had to reach out for God's help, for without it I would fall flat on my face.

When teachers and, later, college professors gave me encouragement, I hardly ever felt I deserved it. My concept of myself did not match the high opinion others had of me. If I presented a spotless image to somebody else, to me it was tarnished.

This was a crucial factor in my inner struggle during my teen-age years. Only in singing did I feel competent and confident. Here was at least one place where I could excel. I knew it, and I made the most of it.

During one of those summers I got a job in a factory, working at a machine making binder canvas for the old-style wheat binders. The pay was fifteen cents an hour. After I'd been on the job a while, the foreman told me I was doing such a good job he was going to raise my pay to twenty cents!

The machines were so noisy I couldn't hear myself think, so I'd sing at the top of my lungs, hours on end, making up melodies and imagining I was on an opera stage.

But during my season as "The Singing Farm Boy" on the local radio station, I began to get hints of a terrifying change in my singing voice. It wasn't coming so easily — in fact, it wasn't coming easily at all. Toward the end of the contract I went to those broadcasts in a state of terror, and the more frightened I got the more difficult it was to sing. I didn't know what was happening to me, but I was scared.

And then my brothers gave me more and more opportunities to lead the singing in their meetings. I was flattered. I wanted to do it, and I did it with all my heart. But in the process I put such a terrific strain on my faltering voice, through overuse and inexperience, that I damaged it beyond repair.

When I realized fully what had happened, that my voice would never again be beautiful, I suffered such an emotional shock that it took months before I recovered. Singing, I had had the power to thrill people, and suddenly it was all gone.

But if that had not happened, I might never have developed as a writer. With my voice damaged, I turned more and more to writing and that talent was allowed to emerge and develop. What at first seemed a tragedy was used for good, and the course of my life began to take shape in a quite unexpected way.

My experiments with songwriting were still tentative. Composing was more a hobby than the focus of my ambition. As a matter of fact, I was in a confusing period when my dreams of fame and glory were still tied to singing. True, the "Song Bird of Salina High School" was no more, but I was developing into a song leader through my work with the trio, and my secret fantasies were taking on a different color.

Ken had become a highly effective preacher. I was doing better as a song leader. Maybe this was a hint of what the Lord had in mind for us. The notion that my brother and I would be the new evangelistic team who would win the world for Jesus was powerfully appealing. It nourished the messianic complex that hid behind my diffidence. To think of the two of us as Moody and Sankey for a new era — this was a dream worth dreaming! It took hold of me so overwhelmingly that it became easy to rationalize my ambitions for myself into God's will for me.

God had to deal with me in a profound way before I realized that the path He had charted for me did not necessarily coincide with what appealed to my youthful hunger for celebrity. And He did it in a spiritual firestorm through which I passed shortly before I was to graduate from high school.

Someone had given me several books to read, among them biographies of Dwight Moody and Charles Finney. As I read about these titans of faith, I longed to give my life to God in a special way. I saw how the Lord had taken a simple, poorly educated man like Moody and stirred the world through him. How Finney was so filled with the Spirit that he could walk through a factory without saying a word and people would be struck down with conviction of sin, simply by being in his presence. Through my mind raced the thought: *O Lord, can it happen again a little bit through me?*

The final book, the one God used to bring the entire issue into sharp focus, was *John and Betty Stam, Martyrs,* by Lee Huizenga. It happened to be published by the Zondervan Publishing House in Grand Rapids, but I did not take any particular notice of that on the Saturday morning when I picked up the little book and began to glance over its pages. In a few minutes I was totally absorbed in that tragic, triumphant story.

John and Betty Stam had been graduated from the Moody Bible Institute and had gone to China as missionaries, where they were taken captive by a roving bandit gang of Communists in Northern China. The Stams were commanded to renounce their faith, but of course refused. Then they were paraded through the streets, subjected to all kinds of humiliation and indignities. Finally, John was forced to kneel beside a block of wood, with Betty standing by. A soldier took a sword and with one blow cut off John's head. A moment later Betty was also murdered.

As I turned the last page of that book, something broke inside me. *How could it be, Lord, that this bright, promising young couple should be cut down at the very outset of their ministry? Why? To what purpose?* Was this what commitment was all about — to come to the end of oneself and lay one's life on the line for Christ, regardless of the consequences?

Emotionally I was ripped to shreds, but I was not alone. The Lord was in that little room with me, more tangibly present than He had ever been before in my experience.

My understanding of Christianity had already undergone some striking changes. During my childhood it meant little more than stained glass windows, attending Sunday school, singing in the choir, being "good," and avoiding taboos. With my conversion I realized that Christianity was a work of God: that there was a spiritual birth, something real — almost cataclysmic — that transpired — a personal encounter with God through Christ.

But when I read the story of the Stams, I began to see that Christianity was even more: that God, in fact, *did* want people to lay their lives on the line for Him. That commitment must be total or it was not commitment at all.

I began to weep in anguish as I prayed: *Surely, Lord, You wouldn't ask that of me – that I go to China and die for You? I could do so much more for You here – Ken and I together – it can't be that You want me to put myself so completely into your hands!*

But He did! Without giving me a clue as to what His plan might be, He wanted my willingness, the totality of my being.

Hours passed, but I was unconscious of time. My tears had long since dried, for I was beginning to understand that if I wanted God to use my life (and I did), it was necessary for my life to be under His Lordship, His control, free of the pitfalls of blind chance and personal ambition. He was dealing with me now on the level of my will. Did I want my way or God's?

At length the last wall of my resistance crumbled, and I promised Him: *Here I am, Lord. I don't know what You want of me, but even if it's China and martyrdom, I'm willing.*

Toward evening an inexpressible joy and peace filled my heart. I didn't want to leave that place, for it was no longer a bedroom in an old house in Kansas, but a mountaintop bathed in light and holiness. I knew a happiness and release that I had never known before.

When I finally tore myself away and went downstairs, the day had passed and evening had come. The family had long since finished dinner, but mother had kept some food warm for me. In her face I saw the understanding that something of unusual importance had kept me closeted all day in my room. She must have sensed that I had gone through a spiritual battle and that the Lord had won. She did not ask what it was, and at that moment I could not speak of what had occurred. But later I shared it with Ken, who understood and gave me quiet encouragement. Like me, he was in the flush of youth and all-out zeal for God.

That day's experience somewhat separated me from my friends and precluded certain high school activities. God never asked me to become a hermit, but fun and games had to take their proper place. They were secondary now; Christ was paramount. I would come home from school, grab my Bible, and immerse myself in the Word. Ken strongly suggested this, and I did not have to be cajoled.

I had been reading the Scriptures faithfully from the time of my conversion, not always understanding what I read but keeping at it. But now the discipline took on a deeper dimension. I was being nourished on the Bread of Life through the ordinary day-to-day routine, and more so in periods of change and crisis.

My family understood my decision. From that point on it was an accepted fact that I would do something in the Lord's work. The family knew it; I knew it. It was simply a matter of finding out what God had in mind for me.

* * *

In 1939 I was graduated from high school. Writing songs had become a big thing in my life. The early attempts at poetry and the tinkering with melodies had meshed, and I was making a serious attempt to write gospel music. There was also the deepening of my devotional life, which became and remained closely related to my creativity. During my daily "quiet time" I kept a pad and pencil nearby, for song ideas frequently came to me while I was in the midst of Scripture reading, prayer, and meditation. When people speak about the biblical content of my songs, this is the reason for it.

The family situation had altered somewhat. Rudy and his wife and children had moved to Seattle in 1936, where a minister friend helped my oldest brother get established in the mortuary business. On the West Coast Rudy also found increasing opportunities for work in music, and over the years he developed an outstanding career as a conductor of large church choirs. His reputation grew to the point where he was invited to direct the choir in national broadcasts of the Old Fashioned Revival Hour whenever it originated in Seattle.

Meanwhile, the trio had conducted an extended campaign in Wichita which proved so fruitful that after much thought and prayer the decision was made to establish the work there on a more permanent basis by the formation of a new Bible church with Ken as the pastor. This would mean cutting our ties in Salina — for mother, Marie, and me it would also mean separation from the Covenant church which had been our spiritual home for so many years — but in all our discussions it seemed as if God was pushing us to do this, and at last we made the move with enthusiasm and a sense of rightness.

Wichita was more of a city than Salina — bigger, more sophisticated, with traffic that I found shocking — but it was still west of the Mississippi, still Kansas.

Life began all over for me with our move to Wichita. We rented a nice house, and mother was at last able to give up the tedious housework that had fed and clothed us for so long. Times were still tough, but it seemed to be the end of the real poverty we had lived in for years. I was no longer the church janitor but the song leader, quite a change in status. What's more, I was now an eligible young man! I knew full well that some of the church families in our new congregation were eyeing me with interest in terms of their unmarried daughters, and this was flattering.

I got a job in the Cudahy meat-packing plant, where my first assignment was pitching cows' stomachs into a huge grinder. Knowing that this unglamorous mixture would someday end up as luncheon meat on a million tables didn't do much to make the job palatable. What's more, I looked and felt ridiculous in my uniform — an ankle-length, waterproof apron that wrapped around me twice because I was so thin and was stiff enough to make bending almost impossible. But at least it amused my fellow workers. When one of my friends first saw me in that outrageous getup, he burst into uncontrollable laughter — and I couldn't blame him.

I only lasted a month at that job — you might say I lost my stomach for tripe — and plunged with renewed vigor into music. When Bob decided to leave the trio to move to Colorado, I took his place in the group. For the next year or two we were absorbed in the work of the struggling young church, broadcasting from a local radio station, and going out in meetings. It was a busy, happy time.

I enjoyed the radio work and kept on writing songs, trying now to get some of them published. The rejection slips piled up. People seemed to like my songs when we performed them, but it looked as if no one wanted to publish them. At last we printed some song pamphlets ourselves — I had the music plates prepared at my own expense — offering them to radio listeners for a few cents a copy. None of them ever amounted to anything.

Sometime during the year 1940 I wrote a song called "Yet There Is Room" which I sent, along with another composition, to R. E. Winsett, a publisher in Dayton, Tennessee. He wrote back that he might be able to use them and asked how much money I wanted. I had received so many rejections that to get a bit of encouragement from a publisher was almost too much to take.

I asked for eight dollars apiece. Winsett finally bought "Yet There Is Room" and published it in one of his books. The only trouble was that when it appeared in print my name had been misspelled "Patterson." This was a blow to my ego, but it was also my first taste of success as a songwriter.

During the same period my brothers and I were scheduled to hold a meeting in Lincoln, Kansas, about a hundred miles from Wichita. There had been a series of services in Lincoln a couple of months earlier, and this was to be a kind of "echo" meeting.

We got an early start; Bill was driving our new DeSoto with Ken beside him and me in the back seat. Just after we passed through the town of McPherson, we saw a mammoth oil tanker approaching. Suddenly it swerved over into our lane. Apparently the driver had momentarily lost control.

Bill tried to head for the ditch, but it was too late. We were doing sixty-five miles an hour, the truck perhaps fifty or sixty, and the collision was head-on.

Within minutes a crowd of people had gathered, some of them snapping pictures. The DeSoto was demolished, yet all three of us walked away from the wreck. Ken had broken the windshield with his head, Bill had bitten his tongue, and I had a slight burn on my back from sliding along the seat. Otherwise we were uninjured.

It was a miracle! Afterward the truckdriver said that he hadn't dared to look, for obviously whoever was in the DeSoto must be dead.

We recovered our equilibrium and got word of the accident to Lincoln. Someone from the church came to pick us up, and the meeting went on as scheduled — late, but we managed somehow, full of thanksgiving for this extraordinary sign of God's protection.

9

Boca Raton . . . 1975

Torrey Johnson is making introductions . . . "Dr. Peterson."

That's me.

More and more nowadays people call me Dr. Peterson, and gradually I have come to accept the title and enjoy it. It may be vanity again, but I hope the impulse is more honorable on my part, for it is an honorary title, given with love and accepted with gratitude.

I never earned a doctorate in the groves of Academe. To be frank, there was a time when I had no desire for even a BA after my name. As a young fellow just out of the armed forces after World War II, all I wanted was enough schooling so I could get out and tackle the world for the Lord (my messianic complex), and booklearning didn't seem essential to that.

I admire people who refuse to rest on their prestige and who keep striving for further knowledge — people whose academic accomplishments never stop them from continually expanding their skills — but in my youth, endeavors of that kind didn't seem to apply to me. Nevertheless, when the Lord steered me away from my intended course and into theoretical work to the American Conservatory of Music, I plunged in with enthusiasm and completed a college course.

If anyone had hinted that one day I would be favored with several honorary doctor's degrees, I would have considered him a lunatic. Honors like these come heavy with praise and complimentary references to what one has accomplished in his career, and sometimes I'm stunned by the gap between what the public thinks I am and what I know myself to be. I was catapulted so suddenly into prominence in the music world that I've never quite adjusted to it.

I've heard Billy Graham say he longs for the day when he can get into a small country church somewhere and just preach. I know what he means: that urge to get away from public pressure and simply be oneself. When you stand in the limelight, people hang on your every word. They assume you have the answers for everything, and of course you don't. Not wanting to disillusion them can create tremendous anxiety.

Anxiety isn't all bad. It stimulates you to do your best. But it can also become so acute that you become powerless. I've learned how essential it is to be able to laugh at myself and distrust my own emotional responses. More importantly, I've learned how to take these conflicts to the Lord and leave them with Him.

Throughout the evangelical world there is a kind of star system, just as there is in every other sphere of life. Human nature is human nature, and despite the grace of God and every good intention people *will* put you on a pedestal if you achieve some measure of success. This is especially true where the performing arts and the mass media are involved. The element of entertainment — of show biz — is always present. In a religious telecast or concert. In a Billy Graham crusade. Even in a small-town evangelistic meeting. Why pretend otherwise?

The crucial thing is to keep this element in perspective. If the Lord is using and blessing someone's fame, fine. If it becomes an end in itself or a means to glorify the person, it's another matter. Since the limelight is the inevitable result of a ministry like mine, I have to try to view it through the eyes and understanding of people far wiser than I. How do some of the old catechisms put it? — the chief end of man is to glorify God and enjoy Him forever.

Enjoy Him forever.

People *need* forms, rituals, and recognizable occasions for celebration. Otherwise we would live on a mundane level. Eliminating this aspect, even if it were possible, would make for an ineffective ministry.

I sense the hand of God in my life. I know He has called me to this work. I see what He has done, and I praise Him for it. The mathematical odds against a career like mine are colossal. It couldn't happen through mere human manipulation. Do I take pride in it? No, it makes me feel grateful and humble. I am comfortable to be part of the music tradition in the church of today, and perhaps some of my work will endure for succeeding generations. Seeing my songs in hymnals makes me aware of that.

But I know also that my career has to stop sometime, and I wonder when it will happen. It's scary to realize that right now there is a greater acceptance of my work than at any previous time. How long can this go on? Tastes change, and I might be out of vogue — passé — in five years. If I were clinging to worldly fame or importance, I'd be in a sorry state indeed. Fame is such a fleeting thing that I can't take it too seriously. God gave me the ability and the opportunities to create some of those moments of celebration which the human spirit needs, but I know that whatever has been accomplished is His work and that if I get in the way and try to clutch the glory to myself, I'm through.

I've always wanted to excel — to achieve — but since that crucial battle when God established control over my will, the desire has been a desire to excel and to achieve *for Him.* During my Moody Bible Institute days I wrote a lyric that summed it up: "I Just Want to Count for God."

> *I do not seek for earthly fame,*
> *For fleeting favor and acclaim;*
> *I would not strive to build a name;*
> *I just want to count for God.*
>
>

I never doubted, however, that He was going to use me. When I had low spots and disappointments, the overriding conviction remained that the Lord would make the most of my life.

To reconcile one's own ambitions with the purposes of God — that's the key. When you can gather all your hopes and dreams, lay them on the altar, and say, "Lord, I know what You will do through me is the greatest thing I can do; the best contribution I can make is the one You make through me." I came to that and found peace in the conviction. Of course I wanted to do something great, but I wanted to do it in the framework of God's purpose.

Lately I've found a subtle change taking place in my attitude — a slackening of ambition. Middle age, perhaps. While I spent years struggling up the ladder, there was always an incentive to keep going. Today I often have to prod myself. This conflicts with what I know to be my best aspiration: to keep producing as long as God puts His seal of approval on my work and continues to act in my life.

When I gave up the presidency of Singspiration and moved to Arizona a few years ago, I expected to take life easier, golf a couple times a week, and relax. It didn't happen that way, and I've been working harder than ever. Apparently the Lord wants me to keep moving and growing — at any rate, I can't avoid it. Pat Zondervan and others in the organization are partly responsible because they keep the challenge ever before me.

I must admit I find it stimulating, and I'm glad there are colleagues who won't let me slow down. Once more it's that human inconsistency that I've never been able to explain: the fear of something coming to an end and the fear of failing to measure up to expectations, along with the drive that keeps pushing me on and on and on. I'm one of those people who always want to be "on top" — on top of whatever challenge is there at the moment.

The other day I met a fellow who said he had found contentment in a certain job — so much so that he refused a promotion which would have meant new responsibilities and a move to a different town. I thought, *Oh, brother, not me.* If I'm playing a game and there's a goal to achieve, I've simply got to try for it. If God didn't keep a tight rein on my carnal need for recognition and achievement, I suppose I might become utterly ruthless.

Maybe this is why the honorary title "doctor" sits heavily on my shoulders — not only because it gives me so much to live up to, but because I know how far I fall short of the image others have of me. Nevertheless, I would not disavow such honors. You don't scorn the love and appreciation of brothers and sisters in the Lord. Rather, you accept the gift in the spirit in which it is bestowed and ask God to make you equal to what it signifies.

And as long as there is someone in the world like my wife, Marie, who knows me through and through with all my faults and foibles and loves me just the same, I guess my head will never get too swollen to fit that dignified if somewhat ridiculous-looking mortarboard!

10

When I first met Marie Addis in Wichita, she was a bewildering adolescent of thirteen (who found me rowdy!). In the intervening five years, before we moved to Wichita, she developed into a graceful young woman of remarkable physical beauty. We corresponded from time to time and even dated occasionally when I followed my brothers on their Wichita crusades. I may have been somewhat awkward and thin as a pencil, but I was intact physically and emotionally, and there was no question in my mind that Marie was a girl whose friendship was worth cultivating.

A touch of the Mediterranean about her eyes — so different from the chiseled Nordic look of most of the girls I knew — was bewitching. It spoke of the sun-drenched landscape of Lebanon from which her family had come. Rather an exotic aura for a girl who was Kansas through and through in all other respects!

If our origins were a continent apart, our upbringings were much alike. There was enough difference between us to create fascination and enough similarity to form the basis for mutual understanding.

Marie had lost her mother at the age of four, as I had lost my father. Both of us had been born on farms (Marie's father still had a little truck farm near Wichita); both of us were part of large families (there had been ten children in the Addis household); both of us had known something of poverty; and both of us had enjoyed happy childhoods.

Because of the proximity of her home to the city of Wichita, Marie and her brothers and sisters had acquired a certain sophistication. And although my boyhood had been spent in town with many cultural benefits, my summers on the farm with Uncle Harry and Aunt Jenny had given me a feeling for the soil.

Marie's delicate beauty belied the fact that her childhood had been one of hard physical labor; all the children in her family were expected to do their part with the truck garden and the cattle and chickens. She was no shrinking violet, though through some feminine magic she could contrive to *look* fragile.

When she was about fifteen, Marie and a couple of her sisters attended a series of meetings my brothers were holding. For the first time she came under conviction about her need for a personal relationship with Christ. Her father had little interest in spiritual things, but, strangely enough, one of her older brothers, though not a Christian, had seen to it that the family went to Sunday school and church regularly. No one in that church ever inquired of the children if they knew the Lord in a personal way. Nevertheless, they did get some scriptural knowledge and exposure to the gospel, so when Marie heard Kenny preach a straightforward gospel sermon with an invitation to make a decision for the Lord, the pieces fell into place. The challenge might be new, but the language was familiar.

All through that week of meetings Marie resisted, but on the last night when the invitation was given, she and her sisters went forward, drawn by the promise of salvation through a merciful and loving God. Then and there Marie met the Lord, and she has lived for Him ever since.

We began to date steadily after my family and I moved to Wichita, and the attraction between us deepened quickly. I was enchanted. In the teen-age jargon of the period, Marie Addis was a dreamboat! She found me a serious boy and looked for ways to make my fun-loving qualities shine through. Whenever I visited her home, I would head straight for the piano, where I felt at ease and in control, and we would sing for hours. Little by little, what began as an adolescent attraction blossomed into a passionate love.

This all took place within the fellowship of the Independent Bible Church where Ken was the pastor. Marie and I saw each other constantly, and our lives became thoroughly intertwined. We were not alone in this, for Ken dated and later married Marie's sister Martha.

Our courtship, therefore, could not be separated from our spiritual lives. It developed in the larger context of the Lord's work. This was a crucial factor, for I had, I believed, given my life to God in a special way and was deeply concerned that my future helpmeet would be totally with me in that commitment. From Marie's point of view such an understanding was equally important. If she chose to become my wife, it would be with the knowledge that my spiritual commitment was the most important thing in my life and that everything else would be secondary to it.

Caught up in the white-hot intensity of our feeling for each other, it was not easy to keep our priorities in order. Then with the convulsion of World War II, we lost whatever small control we had over our individual destinies.

When I was drafted in the fall of 1942, it was certainly no surprise. I was single, able-bodied, and twenty years old. Marie had accepted my proposal of marriage, but we had no immediate plans. Our future depended on the turn of world events and the whims of the military.

My army career lasted only a few days, for when I arrived

at Fort Leavenworth along with a large group of draftees we were given a series of Air Force aptitude tests. The Air Force was desperate for men at the time, and I suppose anyone with an IQ over that of an imbecile would have been accepted. At any rate, I was yanked out of the army and was very happy about it. The thought of sloshing through jungles and huddling in foxholes as an infantryman had no appeal. My first stop as an Air Force man was Kearns, Utah, for basic training — then off to Scott Field near St. Louis, a training center for radio engineers.

After the jerry-built tar paper shacks of Kearns, Scott Field was a revelation: an old, established military post, quite beautiful, with comfortable barracks, manicured lawns, and excellent mess-hall food. Radio school consisted of half a day of classes and half a day of study or exercise, with occasional K.P. or work detail.

It was quite a culture shock to find myself living in a two-story barracks with a fantastic cross section of people from all over America — my first experience of the melting pot. Up to that point I had led a sheltered life, virtually always in the company of Christian Middle Americans who were a lot like me. And because I had not gone to college I had missed the broadening experience of a cosmopolitan academic atmosphere.

Right beside me in the barracks was a Jewish lad from New York who had worked on the stock exchange. On the other side was a young man who owned his own manufacturing plant on the West Coast. My other bunkmates included a Hollywood producer, a telephone lineman from Texas, a few lawyers, and lots of ordinary working-class young men. It was fascinating.

The question of what kind of witness I would make for Christ in the armed forces concerned me. Following the advice of some older friends, I determined to put up a flag immediately, to live for Christ and let everyone know it. From day one I maintained the practice of sitting on my foot locker every morning and reading a chapter from the New Testament. I did it bravely, though on that first day a crap game was in progress on the floor beside me, the air was blue with profanity, and the moral tone of the barracks was an overall low. I got an education in a hurry!

But my flag was flying, all right, and soon I had acquired a reputation and a nickname, "the deacon," though my closest friends called me Pete. Because of my outspokenness for the Lord there was some ridicule, especially at first, but it soon faded, and I found that the firm stand I had taken in no way interfered with making friends or having good times. Barney, the young Jew who bunked next to me, became a real friend. After we had been at Scott Field for several months, one of us was assigned to a different barracks. Barney was so upset that he made a fuss with the commander, and we were allowed to remain together.

Another close friend was a rawhide-tough Texan, Dan Jordan. He was given to dangerous practical jokes, but I liked him anyway. One day while I was reading the Bible I felt something whiz through my hair. Dan had thrown a knife from the other side of the barracks "just for fun." Another time he set fire to a newspaper I was reading, and it went up in flames in my hands. Yes, he was a rascal — but when he talked to his mother over the telephone, he cried like a baby!

Dan had never seen snow. The first time we had a snowfall he sat up half the night watching it, mesmerized. I took him to a concert by the St. Louis Symphony, and poor old Dan slept through it; he couldn't take that kind of highbrow music. He liked to be with me, though he resisted all my efforts to lead him to Christ.

Another Texan, the telephone lineman, was older than most of us. One day he said, "Pete, I'd give a million dollars for your faith." I tried to convince him he could have it for free, but he never did come to Christ — at least not while I knew him.

For Christmas that year Marie sent me a portable radio. and from then on I made a point of listening to Dr. Charles Fuller and the Old Fashioned Revival Hour, the Young

People's Church of the Air, and similar broadcasts, turning up the volume in the hope that others in the barracks would become intrigued.

My gift to Marie was a diamond engagement ring which I bought in St. Louis for seventy-five dollars and spent six months paying for. We had no idea how long the war would go on or when I would get home from my military duties, but at least our engagement was official. I fretted at not being able to be near the girl I loved, but now she was wearing my ring, and I could relax a bit in that knowledge.

My evangelistic efforts took various forms. One winter night the whole barracks sat listening, lined up in two camps, while I argued scriptural authority with an agnostic lawyer. As it turned out, the bulk of the men were rooting for me even though most of them were not Christians. Maybe it was the principle of rooting for the underdog. I had a scanty education, while the lawyer knew every trick of debate and cross-examination. I must say, though, that I had enough grasp of the Bible — and the Lord gave me sufficient wisdom — so that I was able to hold my own.

Only one man in the barracks came to the Lord as a result of my witness, though many listened with interest. I'll have to wait for heaven to find out whether my well-intentioned, youthful efforts bore any other fruit. Some people have the gift of soul-winning; I've never felt that gift was mine, though all my life I've been unafraid to try. Perhaps if I had more of a sense of humor, the ability to put people at their ease and make them laugh — I don't know. In my military days I was young, intense, full of zeal, yet never considered an oddball or a "holy joe." I could read my Bible in front of anyone, let the radio blast forth with gospel music, testify unashamedly to my love for Christ, and still not get a great deal of flak about it. My friends were men of various persuasions, and they were loyal, though my spiritual commitment was one they did not share or, perhaps, even understand.

My most profound experience of bearing witness to Christ

during that period was not with a fellow serviceman, but with a member of my own family. My nephew, Donald Ray, came to visit, and we spent the night at the Maryland Hotel in St. Louis talking about spiritual matters, praying, and reading the Bible together. That night Don committed his life to the Lord. A few days later I got a letter from him saying he was serious about this step and eager to grow in God's grace.

Shortly after that he joined the Navy and saw a bit of the war himself. From time to time we corresponded, and I prayed for him constantly, fussing over what seemed to me his lack of spiritual growth. When peace came, I challenged him again, trying to persuade him to go to Moody or some other Bible school. He listened to me as he always did, for our relationship was more like that of two brothers than of uncle and nephew. He seemed to be making some strides spiritually, but he didn't want to go to school. Instead, wanting to follow in my footsteps, he decided to become a pilot and used his GI Bill for flying lessons.

He died in a plane crash just a few days after I enrolled in Moody Bible Institute. It was a terrible loss to the family, but I am eternally grateful to have had a part in his decision to trust his life to the Lord.

Don was not the only member of my family to visit me in St. Louis. My brother Ken came several times, always bringing encouragement and good fellowship. I needed a lot of that, for I was often discouraged. The war news was bad, with the Allies finding hard going in Africa and the Pacific. I had little interest in politics but trusted our national leaders and never doubted the eventual outcome of the war. It seemed to me that America's involvement was morally right. I did not feel "put upon" to be called to serve my country as best I could. Nevertheless, it troubled me that I was being trained for killing. All I wanted was to be about the Lord's business. I was still under the illusion that Ken and I were going to save the world — it sounds silly now, and I can smile at my naïveté, but at the time it was very real. Strictly an idealistic kid, I saw even the international conflagration in spiritual terms and ached to be doing my part to rescue a lost world.

Writing songs was also very much on my mind. I spent the first anniversary of Pearl Harbor writing letters to various publishers and enclosing some of my efforts. All through my military service I kept this up consistently, bombarding Percy Crawford, Wendell Loveless, the Rodeheaver Hall-Mack Company, and many others with the tunes and lyrics that flowed from my pen. Their lack of response was dispiriting, but I never let it stop me.

While I tried to deafen my ears to the incessant barrage of obscenity and profanity of "army talk" and to blind my eyes to the signs of moral laxity all around, I was also, surprisingly, going through a toughening physical process which was more than welcome. Within a few months at Scott Field I had gained twenty pounds. That brought me up to 152 — still pretty rangy for a six-footer, but such an improvement that I was forced to revise my opinion of my physical condition and capabilities. For years I had thought of myself as the little guy in the Charles Atlas advertisements, the "97-pound weakling" who gets sand kicked in his face. Military life was proving to be my personal "dynamic tension" course, and I was both astonished and elated. Astonished that I could keep up with the other fellows, even outstrip some of them, in the tough physical regimen we were put through. Elated because I not only felt in tip-top shape, but realized for the first time that I had a good body, capable of far more than I had ever been willing to hope. My inferiority complex was beginning to show a few dents.

Marie came to visit one weekend, an event I looked forward to with such anticipation and treasured so much that when it was over I had another bout with depression. We wrote to each other every day, but a letter, no matter how full of love and reassurance, was no substitute for physical proximity.

I completed the radio school course, qualified to be a radio repairman or a radio operator on a bomber, with the added option of taking further training as a tower operator. None of these things happened, for the vagaries and exigencies of the military suddenly determined that all of us who were physically fit would be sent to aerial gunnery school for flight crew training. The idea of being an aerial gunner didn't thrill me, but I was pleasantly shocked to measure up to the physical qualifications and gladly accepted the assignment.

It meant a move from St. Louis to the little town of Laredo, Texas, right on the Mexican border. Quite a shift, from the cold Missouri winter to the blistering heat of the desert! Everything had a burnt-out look. The vegetation struck me not as something which had been singed to death but as something which had never lived at all.

Scott Field's spit-and-polish regulations were noticeably absent in Laredo. There was an almost studied casual atmosphere, as if the scorching heat and dryness had pushed military discipline beyond the scope of human resources.

In the evening the boys would drift into town to flirt with the young ladies — mostly Mexican senoritas — some of whom made their availability all too obvious. To watch the dark-haired young girls promenade around the city square in their colorful costumes — the prettier ones inevitably reminding me of my dark-haired, dark-eyed Marie — was a beautiful sight. I wandered into old Mexico a few times to buy gifts of jewelry for Marie and my mother. But the cesspool of the red-light district, in the shadow of the cathedral, was a sad and distressing sight. It caused me to keep to the American side, where I started to attend a local Baptist church and to visit its servicemen's center where I played the piano, read the Bible, and enjoyed the conversation.

From time to time some aspect of our training would bring home the fact that this was more than an unusual interlude in my life: we were at war, and I was a part of it. Like the day when a sergeant taught us how to take apart a fifty-caliber machine gun. I looked at the gun and recoiled inwardly. What was I doing with this thing in my hands? A gun to aim at a fellow creature, a trigger to pull, bullets to rip into a human body —

snuff out a human life! Why me, when my heart was in the things of the Lord?

Nevertheless I went through the routine, learning what I had to learn. It was war; there was no way to shut that fact from my consciousness. Triggers had to be pulled; bombs had to be dropped, if we were to win — as I was convinced we must and would. But the personal thing of actually holding a gun — the cold, mechanical, brutal efficiency of it — that was not easy.

However, my gunnery training was short-lived. One afternoon I was out for a stroll with three of my closest friends, and we spied a notice on the bulletin board: Wanted — Air Cadets. We looked at one another, read the notice over, and looked at one another again. Air cadets . . . pilots . . . fly boys: the *crème de la crème* of the Air Force! Glamour, excitement, prestige — all these and more were summoned up by the mention of Air Cadets. Did we dare try out? Were we so in love with the prospect of being gunners? Why not?

In a few moments the decision was made. For me it seemed a remote possibility. With only a high-school education I was sure I could not do the academic work. I also had some concern about the physical requirements, though I was no longer the puny weakling I had been a few months before.

The qualifying tests for air cadets were unbelievably tough. They really put us through the wringer — physically, academically, and psychologically. Every new examination was an ordeal because my inferiority complex was once again clicking along in high gear. You'd have thought by this time I would have gotten the message, but I hadn't. Every minute I expected to wash out. I had left it in God's hands, however; if He wanted this for me, I would give it my all. To my astonishment I passed every test, and in short order was on my way to San Antonio for cadet training.

Our training program was severe. Pre-flight called for two months of paper work — difficult, college-level stuff — plus a strenuous physical workout. Did I mind? Not a bit! I was in better condition than I had ever been and was stimulated by the academic challenge. I started off poorly in both mathematics and physics, but I ground away at my studies with a concentration I had never before attempted.

Overriding everything was the excitement of thinking I might — just *might* – become a pilot. Every day was a new adventure. I responded positively to the atmosphere and protocol of this old, well-established base. We had lost our lowly rank of private, were called Mister, and were treated like kings. If we didn't know how to behave like gentlemen, well, they would teach us. *No sagging socks here, Mister: you'll wear garters and like it. Mind your table manners, Mister. Remember, you're a gentleman.*

Upperclassmen put us newcomers through our paces so severely that I wondered whether I would be able to take it. When fate intervened in the form of a change of policy and a modification of the class system, my buddies and I knew only a momentary respite from the grind, for the cadet officers — now the only ones permitted to exercise authority over us — began to pour it on. For some reason I riled those officers (or was that just my imagination?) and kept getting demerits, no matter how hard I tried to follow every rule and regulation. Demerits meant hours of discipline. I set my jaw, prayed a lot, and struggled on.

Within a few weeks I had met several other Christian cadets, which made a tremendous difference to my spirits. Up to this point in my military service I had not had much Christian fellowship. At Scott Field I had often gone into town and rented a hotel room just so I could be alone with the Lord away from the distractions of the barracks. But now my new friends and I would often meet at night under the stars, on the athletic field, or in a nearby woods to read the Scriptures and pray. It was a spiritual oasis I sorely needed, but unfortunately it ended soon when the members of our little group were sent on our separate ways.

One of the cadets in that group, a fellow named Sandberg, became very interested in my music. He offered to underwrite the cost of publishing a collection of my songs. The book never materialized, but his interest was an encouragement to my ephemeral writing career.

Another, more tangible, encouragement arrived in the mail: a newly published songbook from the Stamps-Baxter Publishing House containing a song of mine, "When We Gather Home." It was the second time I had seen one of my works in a book from a legitimate publisher. (By the way, I was reimbursed in songbooks — five dollars' worth. It wasn't much, but at least my name was spelled right this time.)

If my career as a songwriter was still not much more than wishful thinking, I didn't have time to brood about it. Cadet training was a renaissance. I found myself in a world I hadn't known existed, a world of tough challenges, steely discipline, and deep comradeship. I was being stretched to the breaking point, but I was making it. When someone said "pop to" and we had to snap to attention, I sometimes wanted to hit him — yet I liked it. I was glad to be part of the system. Glad and proud.

My attitude toward military life and participation in the war changed radically. They could have handed me a fighter plane and I would have taken it gladly; so much had I gotten into the spirit of the thing. We were pilots now (or pretended that we were), and pilots were, by nature, ready to take on the world. Our superiors played on us with great psychological skill. They had to. We were being prepared to fight a war, and it would have been doing us no service to let us go into it doubtful or unmotivated.

To be sure, when we were shown a propaganda film I recognized it for what it was, but I didn't mind. I was on the right side — red, white, and blue, ready to go. "Target for Tonight" flickered across the screen, and I was there in the middle of it. If someone had said, "John Peterson, you're going into action tonight," my response would have been, "Yes, *Sir!*" I still had qualms about my qualifications as an individual to measure up to the high standards of the Air Force, but my enthusiasm for the larger task at hand and my morale were 100 percent.

Under the pressure of cadet discipline and caught up in the esprit de corps, my mind and body were revealing unexpected resiliency and resources. I was elated to discover how generous nature had been with me — elated, if sometimes unbelieving. At the peak of my powers, I was still suspicious that it could never last, that one day I would simply collapse.

* * *

Then, from another quarter, a situation developed which made my morale take a nosedive and put me into an agony of doubt and depression for a period of many weeks. Poison was seeping into my relationship with Marie. It began as a whisper of suspicion and, little by little, became a tumult which nearly destroyed all our hopes for a future together.

The whisper came in letters from my hometown, veiled hints about friendships Marie was forming at the factory. She was doing her bit for the war effort by working at a Boeing plant, sort of a "Rosie the Riveter." I had already let a bit of resentment creep around the periphery of my consuming love for Marie. My urging her to join me at once and marry me before my training was complete had met with her firm refusal. She had a better head on her shoulders than I did as far as our marriage plans were concerned; unquestionably she was right about waiting for a more appropriate moment. Nevertheless, it bruised my ego that she had put me off, and when insidious little rumors about her behavior were forced on my attention, I began to wonder — oh, how unwillingly at first — if they were true.

Never was there a direct accusation that Marie was being unfaithful. It was much more subtle than that, and it always came secondhand. (Who was that fellow she was seen talking with down at the plant who seemed so chummy?) No one, of course, mentioned that it might have been her supervisor or somebody's eighty-year-old uncle! No, there was always just enough of a suggestion to feed on my loneliness, my fragile self-confidence, and the miles that separated me from the girl back home. Because I was so much in love, every devious reference to Marie made a far greater impression than it otherwise would. To a young person in love, even a smile that appears at the wrong moment is devastating.

The source of these rumors was, I thought, unimpeachable. Information was coming from certain Christians in Wichita — not intimate friends of ours, but friends nonetheless and surely trustworthy. With each new suggestion that Marie's behavior was not what it should be and that her attitude toward me had changed, I became more convinced that there must be something to it, and I began to probe and question her in my letters. To my chagrin she simply refused to defend herself, brushing aside my questions as if she didn't know what I was talking about. That wasn't what I wanted to hear. I wanted reassurance, and she was evading the issue.

I could not come straight out and accuse her of anything, for my suspicions were based on a thin tissue of innuendo. Maybe, too, there was enough grace left in the midst of my jealousy to make me ashamed of my doubts about Marie.

Skirting the issue, I started to make demands which she could hardly understand: she must give up her job at the Boeing plant. Once again she refused, as firmly as she had refused my plea that we marry at once. I suffered as only a young lover can. So much of my human happiness was embodied in this girl — she was, and would always remain, the only woman in my life — and to see that happiness slipping away was unbearable.

The worm gnawed at my soul. My letters became more strident and accusing, hers more hurt and disbelieving. Had I been mature enough to give it some dispassionate thought, I would have seen that Marie must be having her own doubts about me — but that didn't enter my head. After all, stories about how servicemen behaved when out of sight of their sweethearts were in many cases well-founded. I was a normal, healthy young man, far removed from the spiritual and moral influences of church and family. Perhaps, she thought, I was questioning her conduct because of my *own* guilty conscience.

But this was inconceivable. How could Marie doubt me

when I was a twice-born Christian? (Of course, *she* was a twice-born Christian, too, yet I doubted not only her faithfulness, but also the depth of her spiritual commitment!)

It was a mess. I worried over it constantly, and the situation deteriorated. Seething at Marie's failure to defend herself, I at last suggested that maybe we should just call the whole thing off, and she agreed.

Heartsick and depressed, I plunged back into the task at hand — learning to be a pilot — and tried to trust that I had done what the Lord wanted. Tried also to convince myself that Marie was not the girl for me, though there was no way to kill my love for her even after the engagement was broken.

Suddenly pre-flight training was over, and I had pulled through, despite my self-doubt and the anguish over Marie. Those of us who had stood the course were sent to Cimarron Field in Oklahoma for primary training. It eased my mind somewhat that I would be closer to home now and able to see my family. In fact, I had been at the new post only a few days when my mother came for a brief visit. She knew about the trouble with Marie, of course, but there was little she could do to comfort me or resolve the situation. I suspect mother agreed that I had been justified in demanding that Marie give up her job and cut off the associations that were causing speculation. Neither mother nor I could at that point appreciate Marie's position or her confusion over my inexplicable behavior.

Primary training plunged me into torments so sharp that for a few days I was ready to throw the whole thing over and ask for a new assignment — as a chaplain's assistant, perhaps. Our first instructors were civilians: tough old birds who saw it their duty to push us to the outermost limits of our endurance. My instructor, a fellow named Huddleston, was jolly and fun-loving on the ground, but in the air he seemed a demon incarnate. The first time he took me up in an open cockpit training plane — my first airplane ride of any kind — he wrung it out with every gimmick in the aerial bag of tricks: spins, loops, dives, the works. I was deathly sick.

Every day I had to steel myself for a new ordeal, for the mere whiff of gasoline on the flight line brought another attack of nausea. Within days I was handling the controls myself — the instructor still with me, of course — but in such agony I thought I could never endure it.

What saved me was a kind of self-hypnosis. I knew this was not a real sickness but something in my mind I had to conquer. "Now, look," I would lecture myself, "this is ridiculous. Stop it. *Just stop it!*"

Little by little, mind prevailed over matter. At last the nausea abated, and I got to the point where I could do snap rolls, slow rolls, spins, loops, and upside-down flying and not get sick no matter how rough the ride. A lot of the other boys washed out of training because of airsickness, but somehow I managed to get the best of mine.

Having survived that ordeal and settled down somewhat, I could face the unfinished business with Marie. I hitchhiked to Oklahoma City on a Saturday morning and caught a train, getting home in the middle of the afternoon and planning to return to the field on Sunday night.

When I saw Marie face to face, there was so much hurt, doubt, and disbelief in her eyes that my love for her surged up and I found myself tongue-tied with guilt and tenderness. Painfully, haltingly, we began to thresh things out. How could I have believed her unfaithful? Why hadn't she come straight out with a denial? Why would those people have planted notions in my head — what did they have to gain if the stories weren't true? Why did I believe them instead of her? Why wouldn't she give up her job when I asked her to? Why should she? Didn't I know her better than to put credence in vague slanders?

As we put together the pieces of the sorry puzzle, the true picture began to emerge. The more we compared notes, the more obvious it became that those well-intentioned whisperers *had* had a compelling reason to stir up trouble between Marie and me. It hadn't occurred to me before that their motivations were anything but pure; no doubt in their minds the intentions *were* pure. But now as Marie and I worked it out, and as I discussed the matter with my family, I saw that we had foolishly allowed ourselves to be manipulated because of someone else's conviction that Marie was less suitable to be my wife than was another girl they had in mind!

That was the sum and substance of it. But oh, what a tangle of hurt feelings and meaningless pain before we grasped the situation, agreed to forgive and forget, and put the whole episode behind us.

However, there was one good result of this crisis: it made me realize how completely I loved Marie, and it put to rest her doubts about me.

* * *

When I started to fly solo, my spirits again took a lift, and I wrote happily to Marie about the experience. At twenty-one my disposition was still dependent on circumstances. When I did well in training, everything looked good; when the rigors of military life got burdensome, I was discouraged. I was always reaching to God for strength, however. Even in despondency I never doubted the reality of His faithfulness.

I kept a wartime diary, and it began to fill up with entries relating to my devotional life:

"This morning the Lord blessed me so. The inexpressible sweetness of God's presence flooded my soul — O how I love Him!" . . . "Listened to Fuller tonight. The Lord so blessed my heart I could hardly keep from shouting."

The other constant concern reflected in my diary had to do with my songwriting:

". . . I was in Wichita for the weekend and had a great time, especially playing the piano. It's the thing I love to do — play and compose." . . . "I'll be glad when the war is over. My greatest desire is to be a songwriter and gospel musician." . . . "August 25, 1943: Today I took my twenty-hour flying check and the final exam in Theory of Flight. I also wrote words for a song, 'He Promised He'd Never Let Go.'"

Later, during my student days at Moody, this lyric was set to music by George S. Schuler. It was only one of many verses and tunes that began to fill my notebooks.

* * *

The third stage of my cadet training took place in Enid, Oklahoma, which was even closer to Wichita. At Enid I celebrated my twenty-second birthday and also pulled a dumb stunt that nearly resulted in my being washed out of Cadets.

We were doing cross-country flights. One Sunday morning our assignment was to fly a triangle, with Wichita one of the points. My friend Mike, who was also from Wichita, and I were flying formation. I was right on his wing all the way, and we communicated with each other by radio.

When we got over Wichita — with our families and girl friends just below — the temptation to announce our presence was too strong to resist. "Come on, Mike, follow me," I radioed. We lined up over the street where my folks lived and started to dive — two noisy basic trainers on a quiet Sunday morning. My mother, brother, and sisters had just come out of the house and were preparing to get into the car to go to church when we buzzed down. We were so close I could almost see the whites of their eyes.

Then we did some steep turns over Marie's home. She had already left for church, but some of her family came tearing out of the house to see what was going on. That completed half of our "mission." We repeated the performance over the homes of Mike's family and his girl friend.

What we didn't know was that there was an Air Force installation in Wichita and that the general received reports of our buzzing and sent out orders to apprehend us. We got away, however, and kept on enjoying our prank until we got back to Enid.

Following every training flight there was a session with the captain, a postmortem on what went right and what went wrong. The captain walked in, glared at the fifty or so cadets gathered in the room, and bellowed, "All right, who did it?"

Mike and I froze. We didn't dare look at each other because we both saw our cadet careers going down the drain. Anyone caught buzzing or flying below an altitude of 500 feet was automatically washed out.

There was an awful moment of silence, and then the captain said, "All right, I want to know who buzzed Wichita today." Another deathly silence. Some of our buddies knew what we had done, but no one said anything.

Finally one of the cadets spoke up. "Sir, I wonder if it was me. I got lost today and buzzed a water tank just outside Wichita to find out where I was."

That was acceptable. Anyone who got lost was allowed to buzz a water tank to identify his location. The captain accepted this explanation, and the matter was dropped.

But it cured me. I never again did such a foolish thing — deliberately, although I did another foolish thing inadvertently. In Enid we were soon exposed to night flying. When my turn came I was so exuberant over my first landing that I forgot to take the trim off the plane. On my next takeoff the plane shot up in the air and nearly stalled. With all the strength I could muster I tried to turn the nose down, and then finally remembered the trim.

* * *

At some point during this period I shared a far more exciting adventure — a positive, spiritual one — with my brother Bill.

After the trio broke up, Bill found work in industry, but his wife kept praying that he would somehow become pastor of a church. To Bill this was an impossibility, but she kept reminding him that with God all things are possible. Ken was a preacher. Bob had become a preacher and was doing well with his pastorate in the Denver area. Why not Bill?

Surprisingly, he received an invitation from a small Kansas Bible church to preach as a candidate for the pastorate there. I happened to be at home and offered to accompany Bill. On the bus he kept thinking about the time, shortly after his conversion, when he had been asked to give his testimony at a church in Salina. He was so overwhelmed with stage fright that he couldn't even remember his name. Now he was afraid the same thing would happen when he tried to preach, and he was slated to present two sermons that day at two different services.

I saw how uncertain he was and suggested we "put out a fleece." "Bill," I said, "if you win a soul for Christ during one of these services, we can believe God has called you to the ministry." He agreed and seemed to relax a bit.

The morning service went okay, but didn't strike sparks. But after his evening sermon when Bill gave an invitation for those who wanted to receive Christ to come to the front of the church, nine people stepped forward!

Bill was called to be pastor of that congregation and served there for three years. Later he served other churches with great success.

Three of the five Peterson brothers had found their ministry in the pulpit, while Rudy had a double calling, ministering to the bereaved and making music. Only I, the youngest, had yet to find myself.

11

Boca Raton . . . 1975

The moment has arrived. I stand, face the musicians, lift my arm, give the downbeat. Six bars of orchestral introduction, and then the choir enters and the first theme soars up like an eagle. "I love America. . . ."

This is one of those moments when I can't help but be overpowered by the extent of my blessing and good fortune. How many composers have had the privilege of hearing their music performed under so many circumstances by such a wide variety of artists?

I get an unabashed thrill each time it happens — in a struggling little church with an enthusiastic but unschooled amateur choir, in a concert hall with seasoned professionals, or in a huge evangelistic rally with hundreds of voices amplified and rolling out over many thousands of listeners.

Tonight the sound is smooth, with a good balance and a quality of controlled exultation that suits the text perfectly.

We've worked these singers hard all week. My associates and I have spelled each other in rehearsal, but the choir has had no real respite. Putting together a world premiere in a short space of time is something of a *tour de force*, especially when the chorus is a montage of singers from many different choirs.

Their spirit and willingness to make adjustments have been inspiring. We've thrown them some curves, too, right up to the final moment: modifications in the musical arrangement as well as changes in the text.

No matter how painstaking a writer may be in preparing a work, he always finds things that need to be changed when rehearsals begin. The performance before an audience tells him even more, and no doubt we'll discover things tonight that will result in further alterations. To hear something in your mind is one part of the process. To hear it again in a recording studio with an orchestra adds a different dimension. To hear it in rehearsal with a full choir immeasurably enhances the experience. But to hear it in performance and to measure audience response is the true test.

In some cases it's a shock — you find a passage or phrase that makes a totally different impact from what you expected, and you find things that don't seem to work at all. Then you have to readjust your thinking and try again.

A piece of music is not static. It must throb with vitality and emotion, or it isn't worth the paper it's written on. And you never know whether the quality of communication is there until you hear it live.

Sad to say, a performance can damage or kill even a good piece of work. Not long ago I was conducting one of my cantatas in another city when one of the soloists showed up unprepared and gave a shoddy performance. He was a professional, too, with a good reputation and years of experience. At first I was annoyed, then depressed — and maybe I overreacted. Perhaps the audience that night wasn't conscious of being cheated.

Nevertheless, I could not shake off the disgust and disappointment of knowing that our listeners had been given something less than they deserved. Like many creative people, I tend to have wide swings of emotion — way up to way down — and there is a rigid streak of perfectionism in my nature. I would gladly have traded that casual "pro" for an untrained, inexperienced amateur who would have given himself heart and soul to the performance. Without doubt the message would have come through more persuasively.

At last I had to give my resentment to the Lord and ask Him to forgive my own sin and let me start fresh on the next project so that I would not wallow in a swamp of frustration or bear the singer a grudge.

If I have made a fetish of striving for perfection, I know where the attitude comes from. A childhood of looking up to my brothers and sisters, who seemed so accomplished and capable, instilled in my nature the conviction that second-rate was not to be tolerated — at least from the Petersons. It seems to me I took everything with an awful seriousness. Sure, there was room for fun, but real life was a sober matter calling for maximum effort at all times. That I could ever reach Rudy and Marie's level of musical expertise was questionable. That I would ever be a soul-winner like Bob, Bill, or Ken was an even more elusive goal. Nonetheless, though I might be fated to fall short, I had to give it my best effort. Nothing less would do.

Subsequent years have not changed me that much. It's still a serious business, with no time to waste. I see this aspect of my personality and wish, sometimes, that I could relax more, laugh more, be more at ease in certain situations and take things with a dash of salt — but I guess I'll never change.

When I get with a bunch of fellow Christians and the talk turns out to be a superficial yak-yak-yak — who can outdo the others in stale jokes and small talk — I get bored, stifled. By contrast, I revel in real fellowship: deep discussions about important things. Even on a golf course when I am with companions who are deep in the work of the Lord, I find myself going through the motions of the game, enjoying it, but immersed in a discussion of eternal matters. Does that sound absurd — that nine holes of golf can be a prayer meeting? It's happened to me many times.

Minor irritations also seem to bother me more than they do others. Oh, how easily I lose patience with the mundane and the frivolous. And since much of life is made up of unimportant details, I have tried not to let myself become a stuffed shirt, but it isn't easy! Right now I often have contact with a fellow who irritates me extremely. I can't put my finger on why, nor can I avoid the contacts. So I try to analyze the situation and keep asking God to help me understand that man — and myself — better, to make something good come of it.

Let me never lose sight of my limitations, Lord, and maybe then I won't be so hard on the weaknesses of others.

12

Before the war, Altus, Oklahoma, was a sleepy little town on the edge of nowhere. Now it was bulging with servicemen.

At the Air Force base that had been hastily thrown up in Altus I completed my flight training with twin-engine bombers, attended ground school, and took another battery of tests, still subject to moments of self-doubt. Even as I was fitted for officer's uniforms, I had the sinking feeling that I would never wear them.

But in mid-January of 1944 I got word that I had made Second Lieutenant. Seeing my commission spelled out in black and white at long last, I had to resist the impulse to rub my eyes in disbelief.

February 8 was my graduation day. Marie and Ken had come to Altus for the ceremony. Marie pinned on my wings, her eyes aglow with pride, and Ken my bars. As he gave me a grin of blessing and congratulation, it seemed to me that his coat had tightened a bit about his chest, too.

Immediately afterward we left for Wichita. I had my first

furlough — one week — after sixteen months in the service.

Three days later Marie and I were married. It would be impossible to describe my emotions in that moment, or even to convey how beautiful my bride was, her marvelous dark eyes and hair set off by the white wedding gown, her whole form dazzling with happiness. I carry the picture in my mind, in a freeze frame of unfading joy.

We had invited such a throng of friends and relations to the wedding that Ken's little church could not accommodate them and we had to borrow the facilities of another church. The ceremony itself was semi-military. Marie's brother Fred, who was also a lieutenant, was best man. Ken performed the ceremony, my sister Marie was at the keyboard, and my nephew Donald Ray sang solos. One of my new brothers-in-law and his wife were hosts at a reception — a jubilant occasion. Marie and I had no honeymoon, however — just the few days that remained of my week's leave, and we spent them among family and friends.

I returned to Altus alone, an officer now, but without a clue as to what the Air Force would do with me. The answer came soon enough: I was to stay on in Altus as an instructor in instrument flying. *An instructor!* After all my fussing and fretting about even making it through the course! I had the grace to feel a bit foolish.

As soon as I got the official word, I sent for Marie and we established our first home, a single room in what can charitably be described as a renovated chicken coop. The town was ill-equipped to house hordes of servicemen, many of them with wives and some with small children, but after a long search we found a tiny, three-room house for rent.

Through spring and summer our life settled into a pleasant routine. We were incredibly happy now that we no longer had the stresses and strains of courtship to contend with. We became active in a local Baptist church where I led the singing. The pastor, Wayne Imboden, was a wonderfully helpful friend.

Sometime during the summer this church sponsored a week of evangelistic meetings with the Reverend Bob Ingle of Jacksonville, Florida, as guest speaker. Ingle had a great gift for anecdote, and one of his stories made quite an impression on me. It concerned an old black Christian who stood up in a gospel meeting somewhere in the South and gave this testimony:

"Brothers and sisters, when I get to heaven, I want to take time to see all the beautiful things there. I want to see those pearly gates, those golden streets, those bright shining mansions, the river of life — yes, I want to see my long-departed mother and father, some of my brothers, sisters, and friends who are waiting there. But, O my friends, I tell you sincerely, when I get to heaven, I want to see my Savior first of all!"

After hearing that story, I went home and wrote a song using the last phrase as a title. It was later published in my first *Miracle Melodies* collection. There is something about the word "miracle" that has always fascinated me and kept it near the forefront of my consciousness. From the time of my conversion and all through my years in military service and later in school, no other word adequately expressed God's acts, in the universe or in my life as an individual. Many years later a theologian took me to task for using the word too loosely. I tried to explain to him that I wasn't using it in a strict theological sense, and why it kept cropping up in my work. In my layman's vocabulary there was no word I could find to substitute for it.

Autumn in Altus brought the bleakest period of my life.

Suddenly, without any obvious reason, Marie became ill, dangerously ill. The local doctor suspected an ulcer and treated her for that, whereupon her condition deteriorated even more. She could neither eat nor stand on her feet. I rushed her to a hospital where she was put on intravenous feeding and various drug injections. No one knew what was wrong, but it was clear that she was hovering between life and death.

At that very moment we were faced with a second crisis. Representatives of the Office of Price Administration had come through town and ordered most rents slashed in half, charging that because of the extreme shortage of living quarters the servicemen were being taken advantage of. Our landlady was furious. She ordered me out of the house, blaming us for a situation over which we had no control. She stood at the front door, her face contorted with rage, stamping her foot and screaming, "Don't you know there's a war on?" And there I stood in uniform!

There was nothing to do but pack our clothing and the odds and ends of furniture we had picked up during the months in Altus. Pastor Imboden helped me put our pitiful possessions into storage in his garage, and I moved into a hotel room. I went through these motions mechanically, as if I were in the midst of a hideous nightmare, for Marie lay in the hospital and no one knew whether she would live or die.

The third blow came hard on the heels of the first two. I was in downtown Altus one evening when one of my buddies approached me and said, "John, have you seen the new shipping list? I think your name is on it."

Next morning I checked the list when I went to the flight line — I was scheduled for immediate shipment overseas!

How can I describe my feelings of despair? I didn't know whether the Lord was wringing me out for some purpose of His own or simply allowing it to happen. Sitting alone in my hotel room I took pen and paper and began to write.

I'll trust in God though shadows fret the way,
Have faith through every dark and sunless day.
When sad and blue, with earthly hope all gone,
I'll trust in God. Through Him I'll carry on.

I'll trust in God in sickness and in health,
Through days of poverty or days of wealth.
Whate'er my lot, His will is best for me.
I'll trust in God – and then contented be.

It was my way of testifying to the fact that though the world was falling in on me, somehow God calmed my heart and

House where I was born, Lindsborg, Kansas.

Left: My parents' wedding picture. Below: Grandfather and Grandmother Nelson on their 50th wedding anniversary.

Mission Covenant Church of Burdick, Kansas, which Grandfather Nelson helped to organize and where he was active for many years.

My brothers and sisters on the Kansas farm before I was born. Left to right: Bob, Bill, Rudy, Ken, Mable, Marie.

My confirmation class in Salina, Kansas, 1934. I am in the front row, extreme left.

Left: High school graduation, 1939. Right: WMBI days in Chicago, 1950s.

RICKENBACKER

My plane, the Curtiss C-46 Commando.

Above: Primary training, Cimarron Field, Oklahoma. Right: This was taken the week I received my commission and my wings and married Marie, February 1944.

Our wedding picture.

Left to right: Paul Harvey and my brothers Ken, Bill, and Bob.

WMBI, 1953, when Redd Harper was a guest on my show. Left to right: Redd Harper, myself, Dan Ankerberg.

The original Norse Gospel Trio, 1935.

The Norse Gospel Trio, 1940. Left to right: Bill, Ken, myself.

Clockwise from top: P. J. (Pat) Zondervan, Harold DeCou, Don Wyrtzen, Norman Johnson.

My daughters. Left to right: Pam, Candy, Sandy.

Western Conservative Baptist Seminary awarded me an honorary D.D.

Below: Rehearsing for a cantata premiere. Right: Premiere of *The Good Life,* Boca Raton, Florida, June 1972.

Above: Relaxing backstage after a performance. Right: With Pat Zondervan at *Jesus Is Coming* premiere in Phoenix, Arizona.

Above: Marie and I with our children and grandchildren. Left to right: Pam, Marie with Jennifer Marie Strader, Tom and Sandy Catzere, myself with Andrew John Strader, Candy and Rodger Strader.

Marie and I with President Ford at the White House,
February 1976.

gave me peace. I believed He would see me through.

Marie passed the crisis in her illness, but she was still terribly sick and weak. My orders came through: I was not to be sent overseas immediately, but to Malden, Missouri, to be trained to fly C-47s and pull gliders. The rumor was that we were to prepare for an assault on Japan.

With a one-week break between assignments, I got Marie back to the family in Wichita and arrived in Malden on October 28, 1944. Less than a week later Marie telephoned to tell me that the reason for her illness had finally been confirmed: she was suffering from complications of pregnancy! (That raised some dark questions in my mind about the competence of the doctors in Altus.)

I received the news with a mixture of joy and apprehension. The future was uncertain — I could be sent overseas at any moment — yet I was glad about the baby.

When she was able to travel, Marie joined me in Missouri. She still felt miserable, and remained ill all through the pregnancy.

Malden, a town in the far southeastern section of the state with a real Ozarkian flavor, gave us a glimpse of a world like something out of fiction. We found a single room in a small house occupied by a southern family. Our landlady was a kind, good-natured woman. It gave Marie and me quite a start (and a secret chuckle) to discover that one could be a faithful Baptist lady and still chew snuff! Some of the locals were so expert with tobacco chewing that a knothole a room away was an easy target.

The ways of those mountain folk were not easy for us to assimilate and sometimes filled us with dismay. We had a moment of terror when the landlady's little boy, no more than a toddler, came out of the house one day with a rifle in his hand, pointing it directly at Marie and lisping confidently, "I'm a-gonna shoot ye!" Shaking with fear, I crept around behind the tot as quietly as I could and finally got close enough to ease the gun out of his hands — but both Marie and I were a bit limp for quite a while after that.

Again I got busy in church work and had a great time leading the singing, both for regular services and for a series of evangelistic meetings. And that year on my first wedding anniversary the Air Force gave me a chance to fly to Chicago for a weekend, a wholly unexpected and welcome time of spiritual refreshment. Tears of joy streamed down my face as I sat in Moody Church on Sunday morning listening to Dr. Ironside preach and hearing the mighty congregation sing "O for a Thousand Tongues."

That afternoon I wandered over to Moody Bible Institute where the students made me feel welcome and invited me to stay for the evening meal. The next day before flying back to Missouri I returned to the institute and had an interview with Wendell Loveless in the radio department. He was one of the fortunate fellows who had been deluged with my songwriting efforts. He assured me that he liked my songs and would use some of my choruses in his next collection.

For reasons apart from the songs' merits, that never came about, but the experience buoyed me up at the time. I only regretted that Marie could not have been with me.

The baby was about five months on the way when I got my orders to ship out, and Marie prepared to return to Wichita. Her train was scheduled to pass through Malden at about two o'clock in the morning. As we perched miserably on grimy benches in a dismal Ozark railway station, we knew a moment of bitter loneliness beyond anything either of us had ever experienced. Who can express what a soldier feels when he says good-bye to his beloved; who can measure her pain as she sends him off, not knowing whether she will ever see him again in this life?

The train pulled in. Marie clambered aboard, turned and waved once, and then was gone. I stood alone on the platform for a few minutes before walking away, hoping that never again would either of us know a moment of such utter desolation.

But the next day the Lord was in control, and I was able to write in my diary: "I have a new determination to live for God and give myself to His work — and especially music. The future is very uncertain, but I am trusting in the Lord. He has given me Psalm 121." The diary reveals my humanity, too, in the poignant scrawl, "feeling very lonely with Marie gone!"

I wrote to my wife from Baer Field in Indiana, where those of us ready to be shipped out were to receive our equipment, entrusting to her the music book which contained all the songs I had written in the service. I asked her to have my sister Marie play over the songs before they were put away for safekeeping.

A quick transfer from Indiana to Fort Totten near New York City — and then nothing. For days I sat around with a bunch of other men, alternately bored and anxious. I had been made a pilot, which was a distinct honor, but now with my change in status to husband and expectant father I had lost some of my enthusiasm to get into action. Anything, however, was preferable to idling away the time wondering what was going to happen next.

The call came one morning when I was in the officers' club just about to sit down to breakfast — a metallic blast over the loudspeaker system: "Would the following men report immediately to headquarters. . . ." Hearing "Lieutenant Peterson," I took one sip of my orange juice and left the ham and eggs and toast untasted on the plate. Half a dozen of us were summoned to headquarters and told to pick up our gear. The officer of the day handed us sealed envelopes with the instruction that we were not to open them until we were two hours en route.

Within an hour I was in an airplane (as a passenger this time) over the Atlantic, heading for an unknown destination. We had been issued light clothing, but that didn't mean much. It could have been to camouflage the fact that we were being sent to Alaska! Every few minutes I checked my watch nervously, and the instant two hours had passed I ripped open the envelope. I had been given a troop carrier assignment in India.

The Japanese were making a tenacious last-ditch stand in Burma. The weight of the war was against them, and their capitulation was a foregone conclusion, but they fought on.

My first assignment was a drop mission to our troops behind enemy lines, with Dinjan, located in the Assam Valley, as our home base. As a greenhorn I was made co-pilot on that first flight. A couple of enlisted men crouched inside the plane to release our supplies as soon as we got the ground signal. Some of the supplies went down on parachutes, others simply bounced to the ground.

Only a few days after my arrival in India word came of President Roosevelt's death. It was a shock, even though death was now a constant companion, for FDR had seemed somehow indestructible. I wondered, too, what kind of president Harry Truman would prove to be, for he was something of an unknown quantity, suddenly called upon to step into the shoes of an American institution.

The death of giants affects us in a unique way, but it is the death of friends — especially young friends — that brings home to us our own mortality. One death which shook me to the core was that of a good friend named Orr whom I had known at Malden. He was a fine musician and brother of a well-known theologian — and he was killed on his very first mission in Asia.

The possibility of mortal extinction was something every serviceman had to face in his own way. I had security in the knowledge and assurance of my salvation, so I did not fear death as such. My hours on earth were well filled. When flying a mission I was all business: there was a job at hand, and my responsibility was to do it right. Off duty, I filled the minutes writing letters to Marie and other loved ones, seeking inspiration in communion with the Lord, reading, studying, and writing.

Dozens of lyrics came bubbling out of me. In a letter to Marie I teased myself a bit with the comment, "If I keep up the pace I've set so far, I'll be a lifetime writing music for all these words." A week later I again noted: "I intend to put out a book as soon as I get back. I should have quite a group of songs and choruses by the war's end. Besides that, I'd like to get contributions from some of the well-known gospel song writers — Dunlop, Lillenas, Loveless, Loes, etc. It might cost us a fortune, but I'm convinced we could get it all back. What do you think? At least it's a matter for prayer."

At first I spent much time trying to make friends with the Indians, without success. I was never able to adjust to their way of life — so enigmatic and mysterious to a Kansas boy. Finally I settled for friendships with my fellow servicemen and my solitary writing and devotional life.

Predictably, the Japanese soon relinquished their toehold in Burma, and the area was cleared. There were signs everywhere that the war was going our way with increasing momentum, though no one could predict whether it would drag on for months or years.

Eventually I was reassigned to a camp on the Irrawaddy River in Burma, where I spent the bulk of my overseas mission. It was a big depot, a supply area for the troops on the other side of "the Hump" — the Himalayas. The Flying Tigers were there, and the Chinese, and some other groups as well. One of our early duties was to move back the Chinese army that had been active in the Burma campaign, a happy assignment because the Chinese soldiers were so delighted to be going home. Of all the overseas people I met, I liked the Chinese the best. Psychologically we seemed to have much in common, and their attitude toward Americans (we were their heroes, their liberators) was not only flattering, but created a special bond between us.

That troop movement completed, we settled down to a routine of flying supplies across the Hump, mostly drums of hundred-octane gasoline strapped to the sides of the plane, but sometimes bombs. Flying the Himalayas gave me a feeling of tremendous exhilaration. Though I was lonely and wanted to be at home, it filled me with a towering sense of power to be at the controls of a big airplane, knifing through the clouds over areas so remote and fearsome that many of them remained uncharted. The savage beauty of those peaks and valleys stirred my poetic soul: that landscape was the greatest display of God's handiwork in nature that one could find anywhere on earth. And on a clear night I felt as though I could reach up and touch the stars. I kept trying to find poetic words and images to convey the majesty of the landscape below and the endless space above, always finding my efforts too puny for the subject matter.

Most flights were uneventful. Some of the men even found them boring, though the fascination of flying and the scenic grandeur never palled on me.

We should have been grateful for those routine flights, for enemy aircraft and dangerous flying conditions posed twin threats. By the time the Hump airlift ended, more than nine hundred planes had been lost. Our schedule was heavy and we went out in all kinds of weather. Sometimes the gasoline drums strapped to the plane would start to leak; this was really hazardous, for if lightning struck with a leaking drum aboard, the whole plane might explode. When a leak was discovered, it was the duty of the engineer or the co-pilot to crawl back in the plane, cut away the drum, and jettison it. We could see the explosion when the drum hit the ground, and I used to pray that it didn't fall on anyone.

I had a number of close calls, each of them bringing me a renewed sense of God's protection. Once in taking off from China for the flight back, one of our engines conked out. We limped around the airfield and were barely able to land. It was a stupid pilot error: I had forgotten to switch gas tanks on landing — a mistake I didn't repeat.

My most terrifying experience came during a night flight, cutting through some vicious cloud build-ups — the biggest thunderheads I had seen anywhere — and approaching a colossal storm. Our instructions in such a case were to find a "saddle," a passageway through the storm, but this time I couldn't find one.

The plane was tossed around like a matchstick, gaining a thousand feet and then losing two thousand. The altimeter was spinning. St. Elmo's Fire — that awesome electrical phenomenon — was all around. Intermittently it rained, snowed, sleeted, hailed — anything you could name. Then a bolt of lightning hit the nose of the plane and blew out all our electrical equipment. Fear and a sense of fatality were palpable inside the cabin.

Where were we? Was it suicide to forge our way blindly through the storm? And without instruments? There seemed to be no alternative but to turn around and try to find our base. Suddenly we pulled out of the tempest, and there was camp — right below us. We all felt a bit like cold cooked spaghetti, and when at last the plane had taxied to a halt, a couple of the guys got down and kissed the ground.

Our jungle camp was wildly and wonderfully exotic. Occasionally we would forage in the jungle for small game, more for recreation than for food. Countless varieties of birds made a perpetual clatter. Reptiles slithered underfoot. Monkeys insulted us. And there were even a few elephants lurching through the greenery. I drank in the sights and sounds and smells of this lush wilderness even as I longed for the quiet, monotonous plains of Kansas.

Tragic episodes would bring these dreamlike moments to a halt and jar me back to reality. One evening I sat in a neighboring tent talking to one of my buddies. He was a delightful fellow, one of those handsome, outgoing people everyone liked. We had been chatting about trivial things when suddenly, with a wicked little grin, he pulled a piece of paper from under his cot and handed it to me. "Hey, John, take a look at this."

One glance was enough, and with a feeling of sadness and revulsion I let it fall to the ground.

I didn't consider myself a prude. There was red blood in my veins; my instincts were normal. I had known the ecstasy of married love with the woman I adored, and like the other men in the camp I suffered from sexual hunger and enforced celibacy. But to try to fill that profound human need with the shabby substitute of pornography —

"You don't need this," I said quietly, and I began to speak about the Lord.

My friend blushed and then listened attentively as I testified to Christ's power and grace to fill any human void, no matter how basic. From there I went on to outline the spiritual laws we find in Scripture, dealing with man's sin and need for redemption, God's action on our behalf, and the promise of eternal salvation in Jesus Christ.

"John," he said at length, "I believe everything you tell me. I don't have any question about it. I really want to become a Christian."

I spoke about the matter of urgency, that he should not take a chance and gamble on the future. Our conversation went on past midnight, but he could not bring himself to the point of making a decision. He seemed to waver, but at last he turned me off with the flat assertion that he "just wasn't ready."

The next day he went out on a Hump trip and didn't return.

That terrible interlude haunted me again and again, and a couple of years later I wrote the song, "God's Final Call":

Someday you'll hear God's final call to you
To take His offer of salvation true,
This could be it, my friend, if you but knew:
God's final call, God's final call.

. . . .

If you reject God's final call of grace,
You'll have no chance your footsteps to retrace,
All hope will then be gone and doom you'll face!
O hear His call! O hear His call!

For many, like my friend, there was no tomorrow.

* * *

Late in May of 1945 came the long-awaited cablegram announcing the birth of Sandra Lynn Peterson. Marie and the baby were doing fine. For hours I walked around in a state of ecstatic shock. I was a father! Dazed with gratitude and happiness, I could hardly assimilate it. The fact that child and mother were half a world away gave the event an unreal quality.

From that day on a third major theme took shape in my letters to Marie. Until then I had alternately written love letters and running accounts of my creative efforts. Now I was lost in pleasant fantasies about Sandi's future. Though I could not see my daughter, her arrival had given the whole universe a glow, and I luxuriated in the reveries of a young, idealistic father as he charts the course of his first child's life.

Lyrics and tunes crowded into my consciousness in a never-ending stream. In India I had access to a piano in the recreation hall, but the Burma camp was primitive, and I wrote to Marie in some frustration.

"So many melodies come to me here. I can't develop them like I'd want, but merely jot down enough to bring them to mind later on. Can't wait till I can really enter into the business of composing. . . . Looking forward to the future when I can have a piano of my own to play and compose on whenever I feel the urge. I do believe God is going to use me mightily in this field. He must be, for He keeps giving me songs. Now I have enough to fill a fifty-page book. . . . I'm curious as to what the Lord's will for us is going to be."

The end of the war in Europe brought a surge of hope that we would soon be returning home, but summer dragged on and there was no letup in the Asia campaign. Then one evening in August I was getting ready to take off on a night flight — four hours over the mountains and four back — and contacting the tower for instructions when the tower operator said, "Have you heard the news? The Japanese have surrendered!"

The camp went wild. Some of the men broke out bottles of booze. Others were shooting their forty-fives in the air. It was bedlam! I turned to my crew members, and the same thought crossed all our minds: *This is no night to fly the Hump.* The co-pilot and I put our heads together and found some plausible reason why the plane was not ready to fly that night.

Peace or no peace, I continued to fly the Hump for months afterward, ferrying supplies and personnel, and eventually I was in an advance group sent to Shanghai. We were warned that there would be Japanese officers in the streets and that, since our nations were now at peace, we should be polite to them. A fully equipped Japanese army was stationed right outside Shanghai, but there were no incidents.

To be in a cosmopolitan city after months in the jungle was a delight. Some of my buddies and I went to a restaurant in the French Quarter and indulged in an orgy of steak, fresh vegetables, and glorious French pastries. We ate until we were nearly ill.

Nor did it take me long to find an English-speaking church, called simply "The Christian Church," which a number of American Navy and Air Force men made their spiritual home. Typically, I was soon participating in the afternoon service. I was leading the singing one day when someone handed me a note saying that the world-famous evangelist Edwin Orr was in the congregation. I scanned the faces in the crowd, trying to single him out, but failed. Finally I announced his presence and asked if he would bring a word of greeting.

Up stood a little man in a soiled shirt and wrinkled suit, looking more like a mendicant than a famous preacher. He had been traveling and he was tired, but he brought a stirring word. Later we were invited to the home of one of the British missionaries for a time of fellowship, along with Edwin Orr. He sat down at the piano and played his song "Cleanse Me." I then dared to play some of my choruses for him, and we had a wonderful time of fellowship. One that I had just written, a chorus both the servicemen and my Chinese friends enjoyed singing, was "He Is Coming Again for Me."

There were many outstanding Christians in the city of Shanghai, but I remember one family in particular. The father was a Swedish sea captain, the mother a Japanese. When the father died, the children, who had Swedish citizenship, had to decide whether to stay in China or move to their father's native land. One of the sons, Ken Ingren, chose the latter course, and I recall well the searing moment when he said good-bye to his mother and sister and brother, not knowing whether he would ever see them again, and boarded a ship for Sweden.

What happened to the other Christians when Communism swept through the area soon afterward? I'm sure many of them were killed or had to flee to Hong Kong.

Civil war was raging in China. One of the reasons we Americans had been brought in was to move a Chinese army up to the Great Wall area in the north, an army which was supposed to withstand the Communists. It was a sad bunch of troops, ill-equipped and looking like ragamuffins. The Communists, we knew, were equipped by Russia with the best and latest arms. To no one's surprise, the army we moved north was badly defeated.

In spite of obvious corruption in certain areas of the Nationalist government, I was rather infatuated with Chiang Kai-shek. He had given medals to a few of us pilots for our part in transporting his troops to the north. From my point of view it was a terrible shame that the army our nation was supporting was so badly supplied. I couldn't understand why America was not doing more to fight the Communists.

It was all very strange. Only months before, Russia had been our ally. Now we were on opposite sides of the fence.

* * *

In December of 1945 we were sent back to the United States on a small aircraft carrier. The only eventful part of the trip was our encounter with a stray Japanese mine that lay directly in the ship's path. Naval gunners promptly exploded it, to our relief.

Just before Christmas we docked in the Los Angeles area, and I was separated from the armed forces in Denver in January. Marie, my mother, and my brother Ken came out to meet me. I remember walking out of that military base and giving my final salute, mighty happy to be at home after three-and-a-half years in uniform.

I had done my best to serve the nation, without resentment or regret, but now? Now my life could begin again.

13

Boca Raton . . . 1975

Reaching out across our creeds and races, joining hands,
In a brotherhood that only freedom understands –
That's why I love America!

The choir sounds good, I think, but in the vastness of this building it's a rather diffused sound. Not the brilliant quality you'd get in a small, acoustically perfect recital hall. Concentrating on conducting, I can't get a feel yet of how the audience is taking this. Perhaps I won't until the performance is over. Certainly there are quite a few in the church tonight who will be surprised by the content of this work. They've never heard a John Peterson composition which was not wholly gospel-oriented, and the entire first section of *I Love America* is secular. Some listeners, traditionally patriotic themselves, may think I goofed this time, may find it inappropriate to juxtapose national pride with an appeal to yield to God's sovereignty.

If it turns out to be a mistake, it won't be my first or my last, and I'll live with it. But I do hope people will give the piece a fair hearing. My feeling for my country goes deep. It's a vibrant feeling, intense in somewhat the same way as my family loyalty. Not worship, of course; not idolatry — but, how can I put it? I'm just an old-fashioned, flag-waving American.

We've been through some bad times in the United States recently. We may be facing worse. And now, with our Bicentennial upon us, there's a burning desire in me to say some positive things about what America has been — and can be again if we find the spiritual stamina to get back to our roots.

I Love America is a far more exclusive work than anything else I've done. Audiences outside the U.S.A. won't find much in it to identify with, unless they universalize the final sections dealing with repentance, prayer, and commitment. But a composer can't let himself get snarled up in worry about whether he's going to reach multitudes. Of course he wants people to like what he has written. No one sets out to alienate his audience. Nevertheless, the creative impulse is such that what often spurs you on is deeply personal, an emotion which must be put into words and music and released, regardless of what its effect may be.

With sacred music you then have to ascertain whether what you've written is more than an individual experience without biblical foundation. But with the nationalistic section of this new musical I have let myself make a flat-out personal statement.

I have been to other lands and places far and near,
I've traveled the road that leads to Mandalay;
I've been to Rome and Paris, and foggy London town –
I've thrilled to their legend and story!
I've seen their glamour and glory!
But no other land can top the U.S.A.!
I'm just a flag-waving American –

Shades of George M. Cohan, Kate Smith, and Irving

Berlin! But it's me, through and through. I have no illusions about the things that are wrong in my country. I'd never pretend it's perfect. But I love it.

Expressing my feeling this way is a tiny echo of the emotion I felt when I planted my feet on American soil after months in India, Burma, and China: sheer joy. The Himalayas were magnificent, the jungles endlessly fascinating, and Shanghai an exotic experience I never expected to have — but this was America, and I was home.

Home!

It meant being reunited with my wife, warming myself at the bosom of the Peterson clan, and getting acquainted with my daughter Sandi. For a few days I was shielded from the shock of reentry into civilian life by the comfortable sensation of loving and being loved, taking in familiar sights, sounds, and smells.

As far as my future was concerned, it was one big question mark. I knew I wanted to write music, but what was the best way to go about it? And how would I support my family?

No different from thousands of other returning servicemen, I tried to function as if the years between had never happened, as if I could simply pick up the strands of my former life and settle into convenient, satisfying routines. That meant reorganizing the trio and getting back into radio broadcasting and evangelistic work. My old dream of what Ken and I might do together — "Mr. Moody and Mr. Sankey" — was hauled out of the closet and refurbished.

For a while it worked. We weren't setting the world on fire, but we were doing what we knew best, making music and conducting meetings.

During one series of meetings in Enid, Oklahoma, a girl home for the summer from Wheaton College showed me a new book of choruses and asked me to introduce several of them. I promised to do so as I glanced over the little book: *Singspiration, Volume One,* compiled by Alfred B. Smith. "Singspiration" — that had a nice ring to it, and the choruses seemed to be tuneful and appealing. I did use some of the songs and was impressed with the way they were received by the audience. As a result, I filed away in my mind the names "Singspiration" and Alfred B. Smith.

Working with my brothers was a pleasure, but as the months slipped by I became restless, for another call was ringing in my ears. GI Bill benefits were there for the taking, and I had also managed to save some money from my Air Force pay. I could go to school now if I wished. I didn't aspire to an academic degree, perhaps because of Nye J. Langmade's influence on my early life. He had attached little significance to higher education. (In fact, he had been downright suspicious of it, though in later years he radically changed his attitude.) No, I didn't see myself as a scholar, but if I could spend a semester or a year in school, perhaps then I might be ready to take on the world for the Lord.

I had no doubts about *which* school it would be, if I decided to have a go at it: Moody Bible Institute in Chicago. Not only did I have a high regard for the school's reputation, but I also had that vivid wartime memory of visiting Moody and being treated royally by the students and staff.

Raising the subject of school stirred up a hornet's nest among some of my close friends and even members of my family. Why, I was no schoolboy! I had a wife and a child to take care of. And where would we live? The war had brought housing construction in Chicago to a halt, and the city was overflowing with humanity. Available apartments simply did not exist. If I had been single, this would have been a matter of no great consequence; any little room would do. But —

Nevertheless, by now I felt sure the Lord wanted me to go, and I put the well-intentioned objections to an end with the firm announcement, "I'm going." Off went my application to Moody.

One morning during my devotions I read Psalm 50, and verse 10 leaped out at me: "For every beast of the forest is mine, and the cattle on a thousand hills." If this was true, then surely God could be trusted to take care of three Petersons! Confident in this knowledge, I sat down and wrote the chorus "He Owns the Cattle on a Thousand Hills." The Lord honored my leap of faith and later confirmed it by making that chorus the first of my compositions to find nationwide popularity.

But when I arrived in Chicago, alone and scared, I began to wonder if I had misinterpreted God's call. The city was overwhelming. I walked through the streets of the Loop in early evening, jostled by an endless stream of sullen strangers, feeling smaller and smaller, more and more insecure in that incredible hubbub. My search for a room finally ended when I got the last available cubicle in a downtown YMCA hotel. It was so small I could hardly kneel by my bed to pray, and by then I was about ready to turn around and head back to Wichita.

All evening I kept trying to telephone Mr. Broman, the dean of men at Moody, to tell him I had changed my mind and was cancelling out. But no matter how many times I phoned, I could not reach him. Finally it occurred to me that perhaps the Lord was in this, preventing me from taking that step. So I had a time of prayer and went to bed, and in the morning I felt more optimistic and went to the school to register.

If there is any metaphor adequate to express what it was like to be at Moody in those days, I don't know it. I thought I was in heaven. My years in the military had been exciting and rewarding in their own way, but as far as fellowship with Christians, cultural things, biblical truth, music — all the things I loved — my war service had been arid. Moody was a paradise of all that fed my soul and nourished my spirit. To sit in Monday morning chapel and hear a thousand kids sing the majestic old hymns of faith . . . to listen to the Moody Chorale, unable to prevent tears of happiness from forming in my eyes . . . to sit in classes with great men like Wilbur Smith and have them open up the Word of God . . . I was like a sponge, soaking up all the richness of the experience. I knew now that I had not misread God's intentions; this was where He wanted me to be.

I still had the problem of finding a place where Marie and Sandi and I could be together, for at first I lived in a dormitory.

One day a new friend said, "There's a notice on the bulletin board — an apartment available for someone whose wife is a nurse." Marie was not a nurse, but I was desperate and decided to check it out just the same.

I took the elevated to a pleasant area on the north side of the city, at that time still largely a Swedish neighborhood, and located the apartment, a second-floor flat in a well-kept building. The woman who greeted me was friendly and gregarious. Her husband owned a bar. They were planning a four or five months' trip to Europe and wanted someone to stay in the apartment while they were away.

That apartment! I had never seen anything like it — full of exquisite French Provincial furniture. And the rent was so low it was as if they were giving it away. After some conversation the woman said I could have the flat. I told her my wife was not a nurse, but she brushed this aside. She had been a nurse herself, and apparently it was a quirk with her to advertise the place that way, but she did not make an issue of it.

Marie and the baby joined me at once, and for more than six months we lived in high style. Even after the landlady and her husband returned from Europe we stayed on with them for a short time. And how we needed it! It was truly a blessing for which we thanked God over and over again.

Another fruitful "coincidence" took place during my first days in school. In Wilbur Smith's class I found myself seated next to an Oklahoman named Pack who had a family, lived in an apartment off campus, and had just taken over as pastor of a little church on the west side. When he found out I was involved in music, he said, "Why don't you come over and help me? You can lead the singing and the choir." It sounded good, and I immediately agreed.

Lawndale Bible Church, a branch of the Cicero Bible Church in Chicago, was located in a rather poor neighborhood. After Marie and I left the beautiful apartment on the north side, we lived for a short time with a Polish family near the church. All went well until the day I took a telephone call in the dining room and Sandi followed me. Our landlady, who was not too fond of children under the best of circumstances, walked into the room just in time to see Sandi pull her beautiful lace tablecloth off the table, carrying with it an expensive centerpiece. Our stay there was short!

Working at Lawndale Church with my friend Pack was a valuable practical experience, though it was not easy to fit into my schedule at school. It was really my first paid job as a musician on my own. Pack preached, and I was in charge of the music. There were never more than fifteen people in the choir, but we had some good times.

Money was a problem. What came in from the GI Bill was not enough to keep a family going. Our savings soon dwindled, and the amount the Lawndale congregation was able to pay me was too minuscule to make much difference. But we had the Lord, we had each other, and we had Moody.

Soon I met the two well-known songwriters, George Schuler and Harry Dixon Loes, who taught music at the institute. They took an immediate interest in me and became my good friends. They both gave me encouragement in my writing, and we also collaborated on quite a few songs.

George Schuler was a tall, handsome man with a flowing mane of white hair. He was dignified, a wonderful organist, and highly sophisticated, fully familiar with the classics as well as with gospel music — the personification of what I thought a songwriter should be. He tried to help me get my compositions published and was responsible for one of my songs being bought by Haldor Lillenas. It was my first publication while at Moody, a song called "Something That He Cannot See."

Harry Dixon Loes was the other source of my greatest encouragement in my early songwriting. He and Schuler were totally different in temperament. Loes wrote scores of songs, and out of that vast body of material were a few songs of enduring quality. He was a wonderful fellow who loved the gospel music field.

I studied harmony and composition with Mr. Loes, and he

became my friend, collaborator, and champion as well as my teacher. He often gave me tips on where to send my songs and encouraged people in the publishing business to take a chance on me. Later he confided to one of my friends that I was the "most gifted writer" he had ever had as a student during all his teaching days at Moody. It's a compliment I'll cherish forever.

The schoolwork (at which I was doing well, to my surprise and satisfaction); the Christian fellowship with other students; the work at Lawndale Church; the friendship and encouragement of men like Schuler, Loes, and Merrill Dunlop; all these were positive values to convince me anew that the move to Moody had been exactly what God wanted to give me at that juncture. Best of all was the joy I found in my family. And every one of these positive influences was crucial, for Marie and I were about to enter one of the most difficult periods of our life. The financial pinch had become a stifling squeeze.

In the final stages of her second pregnancy, Marie took Sandi and returned for a short time to Wichita, where Candace — Candy — was born in January, 1948. When Marie and the children rejoined me in Chicago, we were hard put to find a place to live. The housing situation had eased very little, and we were scraping along on next to nothing. Our bargaining position was about as tenuous as it could be, and when we finally located an apartment to share on LaSalle Street, near the institute, we had to consider ourselves fortunate.

Fortunate? Well, we *had* trusted our lives to the Lord, and if this was where He wanted us we would make the best of it. But the place was ghastly. Only a curtain separated us from the people from whom we rented. Both families shared a single, grubby bathroom. Our quarters consisted of a bedroom, where all four Petersons slept, and a "kitchen," which lacked even a sink. Marie did our laundry by hand in the bathtub, diapers included. To prepare meals she carried water from the bathroom tap to the "kitchen."

We forgot what a steak looked like and lived on rice. Marie had a sister back home who kept her supplied with hand-me-down clothing in good shape, and I simply looked more and more threadbare as the winter wore on.

The day came when we were completely out of food for the baby. Then a neighbor walked in with some canned milk she did not need — just enough. I didn't have the twelve dollars to pay the week's rent, but we had prayed about it and were trusting God to provide. That morning in my post office box at school I found a piece of lined notebook paper folded around some currency and loose coins — no note or signature. It was, to the penny, the amount of our week's rent, and to this day I have no idea who put the money there.

On another occasion we had no food at all except for some Pablum for Candy and one piece of bread. Marie toasted the bread, which we planned to share before going to church. We had just bowed our heads to thank the Lord for it when a knock came at the door.

It was a Moody student who lived in the apartment below ours. He was holding a platter stacked with hot cakes, butter, and syrup, and he was very apologetic: "John, can you help us out? Some friends from the country brought us food, and there's more here than we can handle."

Whether he had sensed that we were in need I don't know — but there was a feast on the very day when our cupboard was bare. And later that day we were invited to have dinner with friends from the church.

Usually we rode with another couple in their car to and from Lawndale Church on Sunday mornings. At night we took the elevated, but sometimes I went alone while Marie stayed at home with the children. It was quite a trip — a half-hour or more by train — but the fare was only eleven cents. One Saturday morning Marie had gone shopping for food and spent our last bit of money except for a few pennies in change. When I prepared to leave for the Sunday evening service, we discovered that the change left over from Marie's shopping the day before amounted to eleven cents, the exact fare to Lawndale on the el.

All through the evening service I kept thinking and praying: *Lord, you know I have to get home. I have to go to school tomorrow, and I can't sleep in the church.* I didn't want to tell anyone. I just wanted to trust God, and I hadn't the heart to walk up to someone and say, "Brother, can you spare eleven cents?"

The service ended. People chatted awhile and drifted out, and at last I was alone. I stood thinking, *What on earth, Lord? Have you failed me?*

Suddenly the girl who played piano in the church came back and said, "John, my brother and I have to drive across town, and we're going right by your apartment. Would you like a lift?"

In all the months I spent at Lawndale Church, that was the only time they offered me a ride — but it was the right time.

* * *

We were unused to luxuries, but living hand to mouth was a new experience for us and for many other students like us. Did we mind? Not a bit. Young, idealistic, zealous, daring, we didn't have any more sense than to trust God. He honored our headlong faith, though there was absurdity in some of it. For example, we were too proud to let our families know just how bad the situation was. It still rankled a bit in my heart that loved ones had tried to dissuade me from the move to Chicago, a move which I was convinced was God's will. The beautiful apartment in which we first lived had been dust in the devil's eye as far as I was concerned, proving that God was capable of taking care of our needs. And though we were now in dire poverty, I hung onto that same conviction.

Remarkably, we never suffered, though I wonder now whether either of us would have the courage and fortitude to try it again. We were completely in love and thrilled to be together. I was deep in studies, reveling in the spiritual mystique of Moody, so caught up in the idea of loving God and serving Him that I used the walk from school to apartment to concentrate only on Him.

Marie was marvelous. She never complained, and if my

moods ran the gamut from *molto adagio* to *allegro brillante,* her steady, stable personality, her ability to laugh and keep calm, always got me back to my better nature and spiritually in tune. Those difficult early years of our marriage were a foreshadowing of how completely and good-naturedly Marie would adjust to each new challenge and crisis. No matter what situation we found ourselves in, her serene willingness to make the best of it was a priceless asset to our life as a family and to my career as well. Not a musician herself, she always appreciated and understood my work. She was interested and sympathetic and an equal partner in spiritual leadership in our home. I was grateful to God that in the early days of our marriage we started the practice of praying together. Soon mutual prayer came easily and naturally to us, and a pattern was established wherein we both felt free to bring to each other — and to God — whatever was on our hearts that needed discussion and prayer. In that best sense, we always had an "open" marriage.

* * *

I had not been at Moody long when I got a note from someone at the institute's radio station, WMBI, asking me to come in and try out for radio broadcasting. This invitation was something of a mystery, for I had made no issue of my previous experience in radio and, in fact, suspected that that period of my life was over. The mystery was solved when I found that Walter Carlson, who worked at the station, had heard about my radio work through a mutual friend in Kansas. My guitar was gathering dust, but when the invitation arrived I said to myself, "What have I got to lose?"

Appearing at the station at the appointed time, laden down with my instrument, amplifier, and other equipment, I discovered that about fifty kids from the freshman class — singers and instrumentalists — were also there for tryouts. Typically, I hung back to the very last.

Sheldon Fardig, the man then in charge of talent at WMBI, was a thoroughly trained musician, but the steel guitar was something outside his experience, and he didn't know quite what to do with me. Nevertheless, he was fascinated by the sound. He put a hymn in front of me and asked if I could sight-read it. In all the years I had played guitar, I had always played by ear, never by note. But I knew the song and played it perfectly. Sheldon was impressed. He put another hymn in front of me — again one which I happened to know — and I played that, too.

Within days I received another note asking me to come in and try a guitar-organ combination for a program called Familiar Hymns, which was aired fifteen minutes a day, five days a week. One man usually did the whole show, surrounded by keyboards: an organ, a piano, and a celesta. The idea was to add steel guitar on one selection to see what kind of sound it produced.

It sounded pretty good. In fact, I was soon on that program twice a week, playing along on all the hymns. At that time students were paid a pittance to perform — fifty cents a program, as I recall — but the joy of being there was almost compensation enough.

14

Boca Raton . . . 1975

Many things I know could be made better, I agree,
In counties and states and even on Capitol Hill;
We deplore each fraud and scandal, injustice that remains –
But show me a finer country!
As good or happier country!
O show me a better country if you will!
I'm just a flag-waving American –

With the reprise of the chorus I pick up the tempo, and the choir responds with a flicker of smiles and a lighter, brighter, more lively quality. (Was that my imagination or did one of the altos wink at me in satisfaction?)

Yes, this is how it should sound — like a high school band parading down Main Street on the Fourth of July, Old Glory fluttering overhead. It's one of those songs that came easily — a spirited interlude before the heavier stuff to follow — and it had better not sound labored. Different songs serve different purposes, and the light, patriotic tunes in the first section of *I Love America* aren't intended to do more than inject some verve into the neglected tradition of patriotism. I guess this particular song came easily because it sprang from my own instinct of national pride. I didn't have to sweat over it.

There is some truth in the old saw about the creative process being one part inspiration to ninety-nine parts perspiration. When I collaborated with George Schuler at Moody, I admired and trusted him, but there were times when his demands nearly drove me berserk. He once returned a draft of a song with the suggestion that I work on it some more. I did the best I could, but two days later it came back for further revisions. Again I tried, and again it came back. I'm sure if it had happened one more time I would have told George to forget the whole thing, but at last I was able to complete the song to his satisfaction.

Perspiration!

But not always. The person who has committed himself to the Lord and is trying day by day to live under His direction often finds that God has a way of shifting the balance so that inspiration comes pouring down like a mountain stream onto the desert in springtime.

Once in the wee hours of the night I dreamed I heard a choir singing. I strained to catch the melody and the words — a new song, but something familiar about it. I woke to the realization that it was all a dream, yet the words, melody, harmony, and even the arrangement had made a deep impression on my subconscious mind. Knowing it might be gone by morning, I quickly got out of bed, went to my studio, and wrote it out.

A week later I sent the song, "Jesus Is a Friend of Sinners," to Cliff Barrows, and it was introduced and sung several times by a 3,000-voice choir during the Lexington, Kentucky, Billy Graham Crusade. It was a unique experience, as if the Lord had given me the complete song on a silver platter.

But even when I'm laboring away, writing and rewriting,

learning from past failures and successes and applying every bit of know-how at my disposal, I never doubt that God is with me in the process. I can't guess in advance what effect my efforts may produce, but in the long run that's none of my concern. If God wants to use something, He will. If not —

To me, writing sacred music, even a simple chorus, is a serious matter calling for every bit of effort I can put into it. Because I nearly always deal with eternal truths, no matter how elementary the form or predictable the music, my song must say something vital to bring the lost to Christ, to challenge the Christian to dedication and service, to comfort and encourage the sorrowing and afflicted, or to be a meaningful expression of prayer and praise.

Thank God, all these things have happened through my songs at various times. I think of the young couple who came reluctantly to a gospel service in Pittsburgh at the urging of a loved one. They had no interest in spiritual things. They had focused their lives on materialistic goals, which kept eluding them, and their hearts were restless and uncertain. That night Bill Pearce sang:

Once I knew nothing but emptiness,
Life was a meaningless thing;
Then I met Jesus and all was changed!
Now from my heart I sing:

It's a wonderful, wonderful life
When you know the Lord above.
It's a wonderful, wonderful life
When He's saved you by His love.
There's a joy that you never once knew,
And a peace in the darkest night.
As you travel along,
In your heart there's a song!
It's a wonderful, wonderful life!

What brought the young couple to the point of decision and eventually to the feet of the Savior, according to their own testimony, was the message of my song! The first two lines summed up the condition of their life, and the rest of the song expressed what they secretly longed for.

"So Send I You," a song I wrote in collaboration with Margaret Clarkson, was used by God in the life of an actress who had come to know Christ and who faced an agonizing decision: should she maintain her professional contacts or give up her career and dedicate her life completely to the Lord for service, wherever He might lead?

In the midst of her dilemma she sat listening to a recording of this song, and its challenge came through with stunning impact:

So send I you, to leave your life's ambition,
To die to dear desire, self-will resign,
To labor long and love where men revile you,
So send I you, to lose your life in Mine.

The actress fell to her knees and made a total commitment of her life to God, and in due time He resolved the question of her vocation.

Such is the power of gospel music. Even a brief chorus packs a spiritual wallop under the right conditions. In 1949 I wrote "Why Worry When You Can Pray," never thinking it was more than a simple chorus for young people. But the song reached Africa, where it was translated into several dialects, and during the terrible Mau Mau uprisings when people lived in terror and many were murdered, that chorus became a kind of theme song for Christians. Somehow it had just the message needed in a time of uncertainty and anguish.

Accounts like these come back to me, sometimes second and third hand, sometimes from the person who was most affected — like the pastor here at the conference who came to the Lord while singing one of my cantatas and who has since won many to Christ through his own ministry. It's a humbling experience, but at the same time one in which I take great pride. Pride I needn't be ashamed of, if I can put it that way. The other kind of pride that gets hold of me from time to time — well, that's a different matter. It's the devil crooning in my ear that "Your're really hot stuff, kid; nobody else is in your class. You're on top, and don't you forget it!" When I start to believe that, the Holy Spirit has to get busy and set me back a notch — and He does.

Like the time a few years back when I started to get nervous about my competition. The public was snatching up my material. I was enjoying the kind of vogue few composers ever know in their lifetime. You'd have thought my spirits would be soaring, and in my better moments they were. But jealousy was nibbling away at the fringe of my consciousness. Jealousy and fear, because other composers were coming up rapidly through the ranks, winning big audiences and making inroads into "my territory." I'd tell myself not to be a fool, but every now and then I'd get that nagging sense of anxiety which translated: Are you on the skids, John? Will *that* fellow — or *that* one — or *that* one be the new star in your particular firmament?

Childish? You bet. Childish and petty, but there it was.

One day in a workshop a friend walked in, a fine singer who often used my songs, and I said, "Hey, man! Good to see you. Sing us something." He did, and it wasn't one of my songs but a new composition by another writer then on the upswing of popularity.

Oh, did that irritate me! Somebody was threatening my precious position. To put it in the only appropriate terms — I had a sin problem.

In the middle of the night, unable to sleep, brooding about this and that threat to my eminence, I finally came to grips with the fact that I was in the wrong and knew it. At two or three in the morning I confessed my sin at last and began to pray: *Lord, bless Ralph Carmichael and give him a good sale on his new work.* I could hardly get the words out, but I did it. *Bless Kurt Kaiser. Bless Otis Skillings – he's been writing some wonderful music. Bless Bill Gaither. . . .*

Down the line I went, naming each person who came to mind, and only then did I have peace and the feeling of freedom I found when I first surrendered my will to God.

It was a breakthrough in my attitude, though it didn't end my pangs of envy completely. I know we're on the same team, all of us whose ministry is tied up in gospel songs, and when Satan lights his fires of resentment and jealousy, I can put them out by thanking God for my fellow writers, asking Him to bless them, and taking delight in their success.

15

A song comes in a flash. Within minutes it takes shape in your mind, and you hurry to jot down the words and sketch the melody before it slips away.

But did it really come "in a flash"? Or was it the product of years of preparation? Maybe the Lord was getting you ready over a period of a decade or more for that "flash" of creativity, and without those years of living, doubting, laughing, weeping, and struggling it would never have happened.

I sat in a classroom at Moody one day when the lecturer said something that started me thinking in a concentrated way about the grace and love of God as seen in the work of Calvary and about the tremendous transforming power of that work in the life of a believer. Soon I lost contact with the lecture, and my mind turned back to my childhood when I had seen the radical change in the lives of my brothers Bob and Bill through the power of the gospel. I relived my own conversion — to me such a miraculous thing — and the subsequent chain of events through which I lost my singing voice and turned more and more to writing.

My thoughts raced on to the flights over the Himalayas, the spectacular power of God revealed in those electrical storms, the majesty of the mountains themselves, the incredible variety of the jungle, and the star-filled nights of dazzling beauty high in the air.

As these scenes flashed through my memory, I began to focus on the element of the miraculous in all of God's work, creation and redemption. The words of a song were forming in my mind, and before the class period was over the chorus was all thought out. I hurried over to the music building, found a vacant studio, and started to write:

My Father is omnipotent,
And that you can't deny;
A God of might and miracles,
'Tis written in the sky.

Though here His glory has been shown,
We still can't fully see
The wonders of His might – His throne,
'Twill take eternity!

The Bible tells us of His pow'r,
And wisdom all way through;
And every little bird and flow'r
Are testimonies, too.

It took a miracle to put the stars in place;
It took a miracle to hang the world in space;
But when He saved my soul,
Cleansed and made me whole,
It took a miracle of love and grace!

With a sigh of satisfaction I hummed the tune over a few times and then tucked it into a folder with some other compositions.

Soon afterward, Mr. Loes told me he had mentioned my

work to Percy Crawford. Crawford had been in town for a telecast (he was a pioneer in religious programing on television) and had lunched with Loes.

"John, why don't you send him some of your songs?" my teacher asked. "After what I said about you, he'll be expecting them."

The thought that Percy Crawford might use something of mine set my pulse racing. His Young People's Church of the Air, originating in Philadelphia, was heard by millions. Always the dreamer, I imagined one of my tunes going out to the world and becoming an overnight sensation, like Stuart Hamblen's "It Is No Secret" which had broken through the boundaries of the evangelical community and become a standard in the secular world as well.

Optimistically I picked out twelve songs to send to Mr. Crawford, among them "It Took a Miracle." The reply soon came that he liked my songs. How much, he asked, did I want for them?

Money, too! I would gladly have *given* him the material for the chance to be heard on his broadcast. But if he was willing to pay, well, forty dollars would take care of a month's rent. So I asked Percy Crawford for forty dollars for the twelve songs, telling him to keep four dollars as my tithe for his radio ministry. Taking me at my word, he sent me a check for thirty-six dollars.

When "It Took a Miracle" was introduced on the Young People's Church of the Air, it made an immediate impression. Requests poured in for it to be repeated, and the song's popularity was established instantly.

I was astounded and delighted. For once my fantasy had come true.

The secular publishing world took notice, and before long my song was recorded by many artists, both in the gospel field and in the secular: Eddie Arnold, Earl Wrightson, Jimmy Carrol, Kate Smith, George Beverly Shea, and scores of others. For several years it was the number one gospel song in the nation.

Crawford sold distribution rights to the Hill and Range Publishing Company in New York City, then one of the biggest and most successful publishing houses for pop and western music. My song had turned into a bonanza.

Under pressure now from other publishers, I began to turn out more material. George Schuler established a contact for me with a songwriter and publisher in the East named Norman Clayton, and I signed a contract. I was to supply Clayton with forty songs a year, out of which he was obliged to buy twenty. The pay was twenty-five dollars a song, which was a lot of money to me in those days.

Norman Clayton must have taken nearly a hundred of my songs under that contract, and the payment was just enough to help me get through school. One of those songs became well-known: "No One Understands Like Jesus." Bev Shea and several other people recorded it.

I was on cloud nine because all at once, after years of struggle, I had been established as a songwriter. Publishing houses were contacting me instead of vice versa. I never got a penny from "It Took a Miracle" beyond the original purchase price, but I had the good sense to see its value to me as a songwriter in the eyes of the publishing world. Moreover, at that period God was really working in my heart, and I had gotten so squared away and settled on the truth that He would lead and provide for me that there was little disappointment about the money angle.

A friend who didn't grasp the extent of my spiritual commitment couldn't understand this. "You were swindled," he sputtered.

No, I was not swindled. It was customary in those days, as it had been for many years, for a publisher to buy a song outright from the composer and copyright it in his own name. There was nothing unusual about this practice. Nor was there anything unique about being paid a very small fee in such a case. I considered Crawford a great man, truly believed in his work as a preacher and evangelist, and assumed he was using my song not for personal profit but to help finance his work.

What did baffle me about his handling of the song was that he made a deal with non-Christians in a commercial house and that they were also reaping huge profits. At one point I got so upset about this that I wrote to Crawford, asking him to divide his share of the profits with me. He declined.

My bafflement turned to resentment, but it was only temporary. Crawford did make one concession by promising that I could use "It Took a Miracle" (or any of my other songs which he controlled) in any book I might produce without paying the usual permission fee. That closed the incident — and I still think of Percy Crawford as a great man.

"It Took a Miracle" goes on and on. It is included in countless collections of gospel songs and has been sung throughout the world. A few years ago I received a letter from a woman who had been traveling through Europe with her husband, a Baptist preacher. They got to Russia and her husband, who was a singer, was invited to participate in a service at a famous Baptist church in Moscow. The Russian Christians requested that he sing two typical American gospel songs. His choices? "Amazing Grace" and "It Took a Miracle."

It is the song Bev Shea used as one of his main solos at Billy Graham's first London Crusade. Afterward Dr. Graham got an irate letter from a British lady who wanted to know what was the idea of using that song, "It took America to put the stars in place"!

When "It Took a Miracle" was at the height of its popularity, I received a letter from the well-known songwriter and lyricist Carlton Buck. He enclosed a new poem entitled "I Believe in Miracles," saying I was the logical one to provide music for it. I did, and that song also became very popular and was recorded by many singers in both the sacred and pop fields.

In the mid-1950s I visited the offices of the Hill and Range company in New York, and there on the wall of an inner office was a framed sheet music copy of "It Took a Miracle." That firm had a big gospel song division, and according to the owners it was the most valuable sacred song under their control at that time.

The copyright renewal has now come back to me, and "It Took a Miracle" is in the Singspiration catalog. I can't deny that it is gratifying to be able to reprint one of my biggest songs without asking somebody else for the privilege!

* * *

Moody Bible Institute was on a somewhat unusual term system at that time, three terms a year instead of two semesters. During my year there I completed all the music courses the school offered and was in a quandary as to what to do next. I still didn't think I wanted an academic degree, and from the point of view of further study in composition there didn't seem to be any advantage in staying on at Moody.

Marie and I huddled in our dreadful apartment and tried to decide what the Lord would have us do. Summer was upon us. We had to make a decision.

Whatever that decision would be, there was no question that we must have a better place to live. A happy circumstance provided the solution to that problem. We applied for rooms in a city housing development near Cook County Jail, and our application was accepted. Four rooms — including a private bath — were assigned to us, and we could take possession in about a week. Because the rent was on a sliding scale, based on one's ability to pay, ours would be very low. After what we had been living in, a four-room apartment sounded like a mansion. This stroke of good fortune would make it possible for us to continue living in Chicago.

Not being certain what I wanted to do about further schooling, I applied to two places, the American Conservatory of Music and the Northern Baptist Seminary, and was accepted at both.

We planned, however, to spend the summer in Kansas, and my brother Ken arrived from Wichita to help us get our things together. Seeing Ken, I was suddenly and surprisingly seized with a desire to pack up and leave Chicago for good — to be with my family and friends in familiar territory. Ken's face lighted up when I wondered aloud whether there was still a chance that we could reorganize the trio and get back into evangelistic work.

We tossed the issue back and forth, considering the pros and cons, praying frequently, trying to thresh out what was practical, what we might work out together, and what was of God and what was our own desire. The more we discussed it, the more Wichita beckoned. Did I really want more schooling? Suddenly I got a picture of putting Marie and the children through several more years of a hand-to-mouth existence, and my senses recoiled. Okay — so Wichita it would be!

Ken was spiritual enough to know that I had to do what the Lord wanted me to do. He didn't push me one way or the other about this decision, but he was obviously happy that I wanted to be back in Kansas working with him again.

We started packing. It was about eleven o'clock in the morning when I realized I had better drive over to the city housing project to cancel the new apartment. A woman in the office there had taken pity on us and approved our application over several others, and I wanted to thank her and tell her in person the reason for our change of plans.

Ken and I drove across town, about a half-hour drive, only to find a sign on the door of the office: *Closed until three o'clock.* We couldn't wait so we decided either to return later or to telephone the message.

Driving back along Ogden Avenue, Ken sensed that I was still in turmoil. He parked the car, and we had another prayer meeting, just the two of us, asking God definitely to give me peace in this matter or to overrule if we were not acting in accord with His will. Then we stopped at the Moody bookstore where Ken wanted to make a purchase. I passed the time browsing, and as I flipped through the pages of a devotional book one line leaped out at me: *I will guide thee with mine eye.* It was as if the Lord was reminding me — "Don't worry. I'm in charge."

Back at the apartment we grabbed a bite to eat and continued packing. Our plan was to leave Chicago in the evening and drive all night. At three o'clock I passed through the curtained doorway into our landlord's section of the apartment (we did not have our own phone but were allowed to use his) to call the woman at the housing project office. As I reached out to pick up the phone, it rang. Well, it wasn't our phone, but I was there, so I answered it.

Sheldon Fardig of WMBI was on the other end of the wire. "I've been thinking about you, John, and I just want to know what your plans are."

I told Sheldon I was returning to Wichita.

"You can't do that," he said. The urgency in his voice made me grip the phone with excitement. *Why not?*

Because, Sheldon explained, Familiar Hymns had become such a popular broadcast that it was drawing more listener mail than almost anything else on the station. "If you stay, we'll give you a program every weekday at three dollars a shot," he promised.

Fifteen dollars a week! To me it was a fortune.

Suddenly I realized why the Lord had prevented me from seeing the woman at the housing project. He wanted me to stay in Chicago and go on with my studies.

"Sheldon," I said, "we're going home for vacation, but we'll be back in September."

I pulled the shabby curtain aside, walked back into the Peterson half of the apartment, and told Ken what had happened. Not by the flicker of an eyelid did he betray his disappointment. He, more than anyone, had taught me how to trust God, rest on His Word, and follow His leading — and he remained true to all he had taught me, accepting as final my conviction that this was the green light I had been looking for with regard to my future.

Relieved and happy that God, through the split-second

timing of Sheldon's telephone call, had turned me away from a wrong decision and toward one that I knew to be right, I tried to keep myself open to further leading, for I now had to choose between the seminary and the conservatory. A definite conviction came: *the conservatory*. As a gospel songwriter I did not see the need for further study in composition, but I was obedient. The reason became clear only years later. Without that concentrated education in the classics, and without the guidance of brilliant teachers and composers at the conservatory, I would have been ill-equipped to tackle the larger choral works which lay far in my future.

Along with many other remarkable experiences of following what I thought to be God's direction without knowing where it would lead, this proved to me that if a person really puts his life in God's hands and wants to do His will, the Lord can be trusted to lead this way or that, put up a roadblock here or there, and give a sense of peace and rightness about decisions — little ones of no particular significance as well as major ones which change the course of a person's life. I have written about this conviction a hundred times in my songs because it comes directly from personal experience.

* * *

The housing project apartment was far from elegant and without architectural distinction, but it was convenient, it was roomy enough for a family of four, and it was even clean — after we had invested several days' worth of elbow grease, disinfectant, soapsuds, and paint! Above all, it was *ours*. Marie set about making it look pretty — something she could manage even on our slender budget — while I dived into a new sea of studies.

My principal teacher at the conservatory was Irwin Fisher, the organist with the Chicago Symphony. He took a great interest in my work, though he never understood why I didn't want to pursue a career in "serious" music. He knew nothing about gospel music (which was certainly not serious in his eyes), and my conviction that there was no reason to write something that made no reference to God was to him, I am sure, the height of absurdity. Nevertheless he gave me his best. I might have been an enigma — or a slightly balmy young man — but he was there to teach me, and teach me he did.

One day we were to bring in an exercise consisting of a sixteen-bar composition. Mr. Fisher picked up my piece, played it for the other students, and then announced with satisfaction, "Now, folks, *that's* music."

It was one of many compliments through which he spurred me on to greater efforts. At Moody I had had no way of knowing whether my writing talent was anything to get excited about. My songs pleased me, my family, and my friends, but that didn't mean I had an unusual or distinctive gift. And although I had gotten a hint of my potential from Schuler and Loes, I guess I didn't completely trust their judgment.

Irwin Fisher and the other professors at the conservatory were different. They weren't intrigued by my spiritual life; they saw only my potential as a composer. If I could impress them — well, then I had to believe that God had given me something and that I was responsible for it. Like many other young people who haven't found themselves, I needed objective counselors to give definition to my gift, or at least make me aware of it. As in my Air Force days, it was difficult for me to believe I could fulfill an assignment. No matter how often I measured up, I still doubted my own capabilities. My real strengths were always a mystery to me until others sized me up and forced me to look at myself through their eyes.

The three years it took to complete my studies at the conservatory were happy and fruitful. I learned a lot, wrote a lot, made many good friends, and enjoyed my family. Pamela's birth in 1950 completed our family circle. I sometimes felt like a thorn among roses — a sole male surrounded by four beautiful females — but I was inordinately proud of Marie and our little girls.

Those were also years of excitement and creativity. My

songs were being recorded and used throughout the United States and even abroad. Familiar Hymns, "my" radio show, was broadcast twice every day, on AM radio during the day and on FM in the evening. It was immensely popular and brought in a lot of listener mail.

I had many opportunities to meet outstanding people in the sacred music field, and I always profited from these experiences. Early in my writing career, for example, I met Phil Kerr, whose ministry was centered on the West Coast. He was a gracious, warm person who was always trying to help someone else, and he had an unusual gift for winning show people to Christ. Shortly before his death our paths crossed for the last time, and we spent an afternoon together in a church sharing songs, he at the organ and I at the piano.

I remember B. D. Ackley, the great songwriter, whom I met toward the end of his long life. As I came into his office at Winona Lake, he was working on manuscripts. He explained that he was rewriting some of his early songs. "I'm going to pass on very soon," he said with a little smile, "and I want the songs to be in the best possible condition." He was a quiet, self-effacing fellow who didn't like the limelight, though he had played the piano for Homer Rodeheaver during the great Billy Sunday meetings of the twenties.

Another link with the past with whom I had many times of fellowship was Homer Hammontree. He had worked with many of the great preachers and evangelists, traveling across the country time and again. Hammontree was a big, barrel-chested man, kind and full of encouragement for a young writer.

These were all men in their twilight years. By contrast, I met youngsters who were just arriving on the scene and who would later make their mark in the gospel music field. During a brief tenure as director of music at Immanuel Baptist Church in Waukegan, I walked into the church one Sunday morning to hear some strikingly beautiful music coming from the organ. A young man, not the regular organist, was on the bench, playing in a style that intrigued me. Someone told me he was the son of one of the members of the church, home from school on a visit. The young man's name was Dick Anthony.

We soon became friends, and in time I introduced him to WMBI where he got a job. Because of our friendship and close association at the radio station, Dick became the one who introduced and recorded many of my songs during that period. I always admired his musicianship and his sensitive treatment of my music.

When I completed my work at the conservatory in 1952, the station offered me a full-time job. I was glad to accept. The radio staff made up my larger "family," and I was comfortable in the situation and felt I could do a good job.

At nine o'clock every weekday morning Dick Anthony and I had a program called "Cheer Up." We would sit at the piano, chat, and play or sing a few songs. Many of my compositions were introduced on that broadcast. Once a week I emceed "The Shut-In Hour," sometimes visiting rest homes in the area to do broadcasts "on the scene." In the process I developed a keen appreciation for older people, some of whom became my most ardent fans.

In addition to performing, I served as assistant to the talent director, which meant scouting new talent for the station. Despite this and my twenty live broadcasts a week, mine was not a nine-to-five job, and I was free to come and go and to write as much as I liked.

It was a marvelous period in my life. Not only was I turning out a lot of work and becoming acquainted with fellow writers, but I was also meeting almost every important musician in gospel music. Anyone who came through Chicago who had done something noteworthy in the field would end up as a guest on WMBI. My exposure to these artists and the friendships that developed broadened my outlook and made me feel that I had a secure place in their world.

In 1953 I got in touch with Moody Press where Kenneth Taylor (now head of Tyndale House) was director of publications. Through Ken a contract was worked out whereby I would produce a series of songbooks for Moody Press. They were heavily weighted with my material, though I used songs by other writers as well. We called these publications the Melody-Aire series, and people seemed to like them. After it became obvious that the first three books were selling, we were encouraged to try a few more. Something significant seemed to be shaping up — something that rekindled my ambition and stirred my hopes.

Up to that point I usually had been selling my songs outright to other publishers. Some of them had achieved popularity and been used by the Lord. But this contract would give me the opportunity to own and control my material, and for the first time some royalties would come to me personally.

This was important because money was again a pressing issue in the Peterson family. Marie and I were not poverty-stricken, but we were poor. I trusted God enough not to let myself get panicky about financial security or the children's future, but I did have a perfectly normal and reasonable desire to provide adequately for my patient wife and our three growing daughters.

The apartment was now undeniably cramped, and without any prompting from Marie and me the girls had started to pray for a house "with a dining room, two bathrooms, and a basement."

However, mortgagors were not impressed by my WMBI salary. Our occasional house-hunting forays and applications for loans were met by raised eyebrows and polite but firm refusals. To put it boldly, John Peterson was not a good credit risk.

The siren song of a big, commercial hit returned periodically to entice me. I kept thinking, *Maybe this will be the song that puts us on Easy Street . . . maybe this one. . . .*

That same year I wrote a song called "Over the Sunset Mountains" and introduced it over WMBI. The audience reaction was unusually strong, so I made a demonstration record with Bill Pearce and Dick Anthony and started to send it around to various companies:

Over the sunset mountains,
Someday I'll softly go;
Into the arms of Jesus,
He who has loved me so.

Over the sunset mountains
Heaven awaits for me;
Over the sunset mountains,
Jesus my Saviour I'll see.

An important secular publisher became interested in it and offered me a contract. As he painted a fantastic picture of hit recordings and piles of royalty income, my head began to swim.

There was only one little thing about the song — a question of changing the lyrics "to avoid possible offense." Couldn't I eliminate the reference to Jesus and develop the idea of heaven further?

The publisher's request put me in a bind. Obviously he would not take the song unless I made those changes. I had nothing against further references to heaven — I often wrote about heaven — but to take out the name of my Lord and Savior — could I do that with a clear conscience?

I agonized over the decision, but at last I knew I could not compromise myself as a gospel songwriter. I could not shun the name of Jesus Christ.

Needless to say, I left without the contract, and my dreams for a major song hit were shattered. On the way home I felt disappointed but confident that I had made the right decision. Suddenly a new song began to take shape in my mind, and when it was completed it became my public answer to the request that I water down the message of the gospel. I called it simply "My Song."

I have no song to sing
But that of Christ my King;
To Him my praise I'll bring forevermore.
His love beyond degree,
His death that ransomed me,
Now and eternally, I'll sing it o'er.

I abandoned my hopes for easy riches and concluded that the Melody-Aire series was probably where I should put the bulk of my efforts. It was at least producing tangible royalties, while a hit song was no more than a will-o-the-wisp. So I settled back into my comfortable corner, and I might have stayed there forever if God had not used a terrible disappointment to shake me up and get me moving in a new direction.

Radio was big in those days. WMBI had a large, rather complicated resident staff. My title of assistant talent director didn't mean a great deal, but when the talent director left and I assumed his responsibilities, my status changed and my work load increased considerably. For months, perhaps a year, I functioned in that role, assuming all the while that I would be named talent director permanently.

To my shock, another man was brought in from the outside and given that position. I was extremely disappointed. It was almost impossible to accept the fact that I had been treated this way. I was unaware that God was behind it all and allowing it to happen to further His purpose in my life.

The new man was one of those aggressive, fast-talking types, full of grandiose ideas and projects. He was amiable enough, but my pride had been injured, and having to be polite as I worked with him every day was pouring salt into the wound.

One evening he and his wife were together with Marie and me in a social situation, and he began to tease me about something: innocently, having fun, not realizing that I was deeply hurt by his remarks. I could not respond except to turn my feelings inward, and when I got home that night I felt utterly demolished. I sat in our little apartment wondering why the Lord would allow this, quite sure that He had abandoned me and that I was on the shelf forever. Satan was humming in my ear again, fanning the flames of resentment.

At last the thought came: *God understands. He knows I'm suffering. I'm not alone in this.* I went to the piano and sketched out a song, "No One Understands Like Jesus." With that my pride broke and the poisonous self-pity and ill-will began to drain out of my soul. Eventually I was able to regard the new talent director not as a usurper but as a real friend.

I'm sorry for people who don't have the experience of seeing God at work in their lives! It makes me sad to think of those who never know what it is to be brought low, crushed in spirit and thrown back into the everlasting arms for renewal and true security! When it happens, you get into the larger context of life; you know that God is up to something, that you're moving somewhere, and that life is not just a helter-skelter experience.

So I accepted the chastening of being passed over, and God used it to bring me to a new dependence on Him. He did not, however, let me sink back into that cozy corner where I had been hiding. My attitude toward the radio station and my place in it were never the same after that. I was ready for the next step.

At that point, Al Smith walked into my office and into my life.

16

Boca Raton . . . 1975

Now our young soloist is taking his place at the microphone to sing "Johnny Bull," the Yankee Doodle-type tune we've put in to recall the period of the American revolution. He seems nervous. We should have given him some extra rehearsal.

There — he fluffed a whole line. Don't feel bad, young fellow. An audience is always willing to forgive a mistake. What they won't forgive so readily is the bravado that tries to cover up poor preparation, and they can usually spot it all too easily.

He's back on the track. I'll have to find something to say to him after the performance to ease his embarrassment. It wasn't a bad error, and I know very well what it is to fluff a performance.

Like the time I played Cleopatra — yes, Cleopatra. It was a school musical back in Salina, and I was still a boy soprano. In those more innocent days, audiences easily accepted the practice of boys singing girls' parts and vice versa. I had a good soprano so I got the role; it was as simple as that.

Quite a flashy part, too, in a modern-dress version of the Cleopatra story. (Did we *really* do that? You bet we did!) I played the Egyptian queen in the costume of a twentieth-century lady, right down to high heels. Those heels were hard for a boy to manage, not to mention the fact that the shoes were too tight to begin with. During a scene change I hurried backstage in the school auditorium, kicked off the shoes, and curled my toes in relief.

Suddenly I heard my next cue. No time to think: get back on stage and start singing.

You guessed it — the shoes were still in the wings somewhere, and there I stood in front of a tittering audience with my big bare feet prominently on display. Not too regal!

Hey, I just missed a choir cue!

Sorry, ladies and gentlemen — but at least this time I've got my shoes on.

17

Alfred B. Smith was innovative in the gospel music field. Just before and during World War II, while he was a student at Wheaton College, Youth for Christ was coming to the fore and the Saturday night rallies were sweeping the country. Al put together a thirty-two page collection of choruses popular in the Youth for Christ movement and published it; the Wheaton students carried it home to their churches, and the book took off like a prairie fire.

Then came a second book, and a third. They launched Al as a publisher and became the foundation for the Singspiration Publishing Company.

He was also a sensational song leader, in great demand. When a then-obscure evangelist named Billy Graham asked Al to join his team, he respectfully but decisively declined!

Singspiration assumed greater and greater importance. Al himself didn't know much about harmony or the technical aspects of songwriting and had to rely on music editors —

Herman Voss was one of the first; later there were others — but he had an instinct for producing songbooks that people enjoyed.

Even before I came to Moody as a student, I sent Al Smith my chorus "He Owns the Cattle on a Thousand Hills"; he included it in one of his books, and it was introduced at a Sunday school convention in Chicago. Sometime in 1949 or '50 I heard it sung by a throng of 10,000 young people broadcasting from Madison Square Garden during a Jack Wyrtzen Word of Life Rally. What a thrill — to hear my chorus performed on that mammoth scale!

Al was aware of me, and when our paths crossed the conversation always turned to songwriting. Like the time he came into my office on the tenth floor of Crowell Hall during Moody Bible Institute's Founder's Week Conference, just after leading the crowd in Fanny Crosby's hymn "All the Way My Saviour Leads Me." He suggested I use the last line of the hymn, "Jesus led me all the way," as the title for a new song. I jotted it down and promised to think about it. Several months later I completed the song and sent it to Al, who introduced it himself at the next Founder's Week Conference.

When Al sought me out in my WMBI office in 1955, it was to inquire whether he could buy some more of my material. Singspiration was well established by then, with headquarters in Montrose, Pennsylvania. The songbooks were distributed by the Zondervan brothers, Pat and Bernie, through their Zondervan Publishing House in Grand Rapids, Michigan.

I hesitated to sell any more of my material outright, for I had my own Melody-Aire series going through Moody Press, but Al was persuasive, and at length I agreed to give him ten or twelve pieces. He wrote out a check for a thousand dollars, the most money I had ever received at one time from the sale of my compositions. That check made quite an impression on my family. Some of our Kansas kinfolk were visiting us at the time, and we passed it around almost in disbelief.

Shortly, Al came back with another, more startling proposal. Would I consider moving east and becoming his music editor at Singspiration?

The suggestion was so unexpected that I was completely stumped for a response. Though I had been passed over for the job I expected to get, I loved Moody and the people I worked with, and I knew my position there was unassailable.

What's more, Marie and I were at last within sight of acquiring our own house through the help of a Chicago businessman who was a Christian and who knew of our financial plight. He had worked out a deal for us to buy a home in Oak Park — an older home, far from beautiful (actually, Marie hated it, though she never told me so till long afterward), but adequate. The thought of being able to install my family in a house that would belong to us was nearly irresistible.

Then along came Al Smith with his offer.

Marie and I prayed about it for months, weighing the decision, tilting this way and that. I sensed that God was trying to get me started in a new direction. His purpose for my life seemed to be coming into clearer focus, especially with regard to my writing. Many of my songs had found acceptance on a wide scale. I began to comprehend that what I had dreamed about for years might now be coming to pass and that the best way to accomplish it would be to launch out in publishing.

Finally we said yes, worked out a financial arrangement with Al, and moved to Montrose.

* * *

Montrose, Pennsylvania: a combination "Main Street" and "Peyton Place" behind a veneer of white clapboard and green shutters! Sleepy, tree-lined streets; farmers coming to town for tall tales and small talk; haircuts, fifty cents; ring the operator to place a telephone call ("I don't think Bill's home today. He went to Binghamton, but I'll try his house if you want.").

Marie and I looked around and wondered if we had stepped into the nineteenth century. What a change of pace after the hurly-burly of Chicago!

Al's rosy description of the apartment waiting for us did not quite jibe with reality. It was a worn, upstairs-back affair with linoleum on the floor and no furniture. Refusing to be discouraged, we went house-hunting instead.

A white, two-story frame house on the town's main avenue looked inviting on the outside. Inside, it was a shambles, filthy, in a shocking state of disrepair, with cartons of empty liquor bottles stacked everywhere. The owner, a lady from a distinguished family which had once served the nation in the diplomatic corps, had let her breeding and European education sink into a pool of alcohol. We pitied her and understood immediately that she was no longer able to maintain her once-beautiful home.

At any rate, the price was right: $8500 for the house, shambles thrown in!

We cashed in the U.S. savings bonds we had managed to hold on to, floated a loan, and closed the deal. Before we finished, we had sunk another $10,000 into repairs and renovation, but the house was lovely. We bought stacks of interior decorating magazines and planned the whole thing ourselves. Marie had the time of her life picking out carpets and color schemes, buying fabrics and making drapes.

The look on the faces of our little girls the night we moved in made every bit of effort and expense worthwhile. They ran upstairs and down in sheer delight. Yes, there was a dining room (sunken, too!); yes, there was a basement; yes, there were two bathrooms. Their prayers had been answered down to the last detail. What's more, there was a bedroom for each of them. If dad wondered about how he would pay heating bills through the long, cold Pennsylvania winter — well, God had never let us down yet.

Christmas Eve came, for us, like others, a time of joy and celebration. In my zeal for the Lord, some would have felt I went overboard in playing down the secular aspects of the holiday. We exchanged gifts but never spun tales of Santa Claus, for I felt that if we were honest with the children in little things, later they would trust and believe us in bigger issues. We looked forward to Christmas day when we would celebrate the Lord's birthday by reading the Christmas story, praying, and experiencing the pure happiness of simply being together in a family quiet time.

But in the middle of the night I was shaken awake by the ringing of the telephone and the message that my mother had died.

Before we had time to let the impact of our loss sink in, Marie and I had bundled the children into the car and set out for Wichita. We drove without stopping, my mind awhirl with memories, grief, love, and joy in the knowledge that mother was safe with the Lord. Arriving just in time for the evening service at Ken's church, we walked in to find Bob leading the congregation in the song, "Tell Mother I'll Be There." My throat tightened with emotion, but even at that moment I could hear the note of triumph in the song.

Less than a month later I was able to write in a round-robin letter to my sisters and brothers and various other kinfolk: "I'm sure that all our future Christmases will be heavy with memories of a wonderful and precious mother. But, say, aren't you glad that we're linked up with an ever-living Savior who has defeated death and the grave and who has assured us of a happy reunion 'over there'?"

In His inimitable way, the Lord had been able to touch our natural grief with the triumph of the Resurrection.

* * *

Al Smith was the guiding light of Singspiration — the entrepreneur. I was responsible for making artistic decisions, editing and writing music. Harold DeCou, a talented young organist, had also joined the company. He had been traveling with evangelist George Sweeting (now the president of Moody Bible Institute) and had been a guest on one of my programs at WMBI, so we were not entirely strangers. His duties were to assist me with editing and arranging, as well as to play the organ for recordings and for the radio programs Al hoped to produce. Harold and I did start a program called "Silver Strings," with guitar and organ, that was aired over WPEL, the local radio station, and eventually over a number of other stations. Harold's first term of service with us turned out to be brief, but he and I remained close friends. I admired his work and kept him in mind for possible future assignments.

Singspiration was a thriving concern, with excellent prospects for further expansion and development. Songbooks were being produced, the Zondervan people were distributing them, and they were selling by the tens of thousands. I retained my own little sideline with Moody Press, but the great bulk of my efforts went into Singspiration.

I had corresponded with the Zondervan brothers, but the opportunity to meet them in person did not come until they invited me to Grand Rapids for the silver anniversary of the founding of the Zondervan Publishing House. Driving toward Grand Rapids, I felt a mixture of anticipation and apprehension. Pat and Bernie Zondervan had the reputation of being superefficient businessmen who worked hard, kept a short rein on their commercial interests, and rarely made a wrong move. Perhaps I feared that they would be cold-hearted and "all business."

But when I walked down the hallway toward Pat's office and he came out to greet me with a big smile and a hearty, "John, it's a delight to meet you!", I knew my fears had been groundless. Bernie proved to have the same warmth, the same great heart, the same deep love of music. I had found two priceless men who would be my friends throughout eternity.

Living in Montrose, far from the mainstream of activity in the Publishing business, had some awkward disadvantages, but there were advantages, too. Our proximity to the Montrose Bible Conference, founded many years before by the evangelist R. A. Torrey, proved to be beneficial. Our family often attended the meetings, and I became active in the music program. The Reverend W. Douglas Roe, at that time conference director, and his wife Natalie became our good friends.

Eventually I was made a member of the conference board, serving with some outstanding Christian businessmen and with such gifted individuals as William Ward Ayer, Harold Laird, and R. A. Torrey, Jr. We also had rewarding contacts with the preachers and musicians who graced the conference platform, and our home frequently became the scene of after-service conversation with these visiting personalities. It was here, for example, that I first met Oswald J. Smith, and a songwriting collaboration and friendship began that has endured through the years.

Activities like these, which enriched my spiritual life and stretched my horizons, had to be made to fit around my main responsibilities centered in the Singspiration office. There was a constant demand for new material, and soon another need became obvious among the people and churches we served: a need for choral music — choral music with strong evangelical texts, and with attractive and singable arrangements that could be learned quickly and performed capably by even a small group of volunteer singers. Another company had made a beachhead in this area, but it did not begin to meet the demand. We convinced ourselves that Singspiration's strong scriptural emphasis would enhance our product and perhaps reach a larger audience.

Coincidentally, a gentleman came to Al with some ideas for music that would fill the very needs we had been discussing, and Al got fired up with the idea of starting a new company. In due course the new man joined our team, a small company he had organized previously was absorbed, and Better Choirs was founded. Our new colleague was put in charge of the effort, and we began to produce a steady stream of choral items.

The operation was soon moved to Minneapolis where our main printing was done. Only the editing, which I supervised, was handled in the Montrose office. The concept seemed eminently workable, and the Better Choirs material sold very well.

Moving into choral music filled me with trepidation. Never had I thought of myself as a choral writer. As a student at Moody I did not have much interest in arranging choir music. And although at the conservatory I had had to compose in music forms larger than the song style which was so familiar to me, the emphasis was more instrumental than choral. Then the failure in one of my early choral conducting jobs further diminished my confidence. Now in Montrose I had no choice but to start doing pieces for choir, and little by little I began to feel at ease in the medium.

I could see that my choral compositions were fair enough, but it never occurred to me that my talent lay anywhere but in straight gospel songwriting. This conviction was further deepened when Al and I were summoned to the offices of Hill and Range Songs in New York City during the summer of 1956.

The men who ran Hill and Range, two Jewish brothers originally from Europe, were anxious to have some of my songs. "It Took a Miracle," which they controlled by virtue of their deal with Percy Crawford, was an enormously valuable property, and they were eager to try again for the kind of popularity it enjoyed.

They received us as if we were nobility, and as they spoke glowingly of what we might do together, combining my songwriting with their merchandising abilities, I found myself flattered, impressed, and intrigued. Another advantage of an arrangement with Hill and Range would be that they would assist me in becoming a writer-member of Broadcast Music, Inc. (BMI). Since Hill and Range was a BMI company and "It Took a Miracle" was in the BMI catalog, I would at last receive performance fees for its use on radio and TV.

An appointment was secured with BMI people. After some discussion, a contract was prepared which called for an immediate payment of some back performance money. I was fascinated and even excited when these negotiations started, but I soon became uncomfortable and uneasy. Somehow I did not have peace in my heart about the proceedings. Just as I was ready to sign the contract, having pen in hand, I suddenly turned to their lawyer and declined the offer.

Singspiration, and therefore most of my music up to that time, was affiliated with SESAC, a rival performing society. Al Smith had agreed to my personal foray into BMI, hoping that the contact might somehow be valuable to us in the future.

Back at Hill and Range, my decision regarding BMI was accepted. When a song contract was drawn up — a contract covering about twelve of my tunes — it contained a clause recognizing the prior claim of SESAC to represent the songs in question for TV, radio, and recordings. This seemed to satisfy everyone, and we signed.

It all happened fast, with optimism and good will. But in the months to follow, and in spite of recordings Hill and Range had secured for several of my songs, I became more and more apprehensive about what I had done. My uneasiness was caused by a revolution in the pop music field. A young man named Elvis Presley had appeared on the scene and captivated the nation. Suddenly everything was "rock-and-roll," and there wasn't a Tin-Pan Alley firm that didn't try to cash in on the trend — Hill and Range included.

The thought of what might happen terrified me — a John Peterson gospel song with a rock-and-roll arrangement? I castigated myself for succumbing to the temptation of the "big time."

Confused and doubtful, I determined to attempt dissolving the contract and was eventually able to do so and secure my songs back on the basis of that clause relating to the prior claims of SESAC.

I felt bad about letting down people who were counting on me, but I was relieved to have gotten out of a potentially compromising situation. And I determined from then on to be very careful in dealings with secular publishers.

That decision, though a right one for me, did nothing to spare me from a far more complicated and agonizing business entanglement which was brewing and which ended in disillusionment and shattered hopes for some who were near and dear to me.

Before the storm broke, however, there were months of feverish productivity and one outstanding breakthrough in our creative and publishing venture, the implications and ramifications of which no one could foresee.

One day during a Better Choirs staff meeting we were discussing the choir needs of the nation and talking about the arrangements and anthems we had produced. Suddenly someone said, "Along with these things we ought to produce a cantata."

The room became quiet. Nothing was said, but I could sense that the others were looking at me.

A cantata? That was the furthest thing from my mind. I had never considered such a project — didn't even know how to begin. What's more, I was then consumed with an ambition to write a Broadway musical, a Christian Broadway musical. I certainly didn't want to be diverted from that project, which I felt had a lot of potential.

But I thought and prayed about a cantata and finally came up with something based on the old Bliss hymn "Hallelujah, What a Saviour." Frankly, I was feeling my way, but I did have a pattern in mind. I wanted to set forth the resurrection story in a combination of narration and singing. Another thing: I introduced a recurring musical theme which, along with the narration, would give continuity to the work.

With little confidence in the undertaking, I completed the work. A choir demonstration record was made in Minneapolis under the direction of Jim Davies, director of music at the First Covenant Church in that city, using an excellent semiprofessional musical group called the Minneapolis Choralaires. I was surprised by the enthusiastic reception it got. The combination demo-record and cantata book introduced a new kind of marketing which we have used ever since with great success.

Then one day I walked into my Montrose office and noticed an artist's sketch for a new book cover. It was the proposed cover design for a Christmas cantata to be called "Love Transcending" — and my name was on it. Because of the success of "Hallelujah, What a Saviour," my colleagues felt I should write another cantata at once, and they had instructed our artist to prepare the cover without telling me. I got the message and completed the work.

It was a smash. I couldn't believe it! Choir directors were buying it in great quantities, and letters of appreciation came pouring in. Somehow we had hit on a combination that captured people's imagination — maybe because I was a writer of melody, and these two cantatas were very melodic.

With these full-length compositions plus my regular duties, my work schedule grew heavier. But from time to time there would be an unusually happy interlude to buoy my spirits. In June of 1957 I wrote to my family: "Yesterday we were in New York — had lunch with Cliff Barrows, Bev Shea, Paul Mickelson, and Tedd Smith of the Graham team — all of them are terrific guys. Attended the rally in Madison Square Garden last night — words are inadequate to describe it. Bev sang 'It Took a Miracle.' Cliff made mention of my presence in the audience. It was a wonderful day."

For Christmas in 1958 I wrote the cantata, "Night of Miracles"; its instantaneous acceptance dwarfed the popularity of the two earlier works and literally stunned me with its magnitude. Its release brought letters and telegrams from people all across America. Friends and even strangers began to send newspaper clippings showing church schedules of musical programs and services; it was not unusual to find scores of churches in a single city doing one or another of my cantatas on a holiday weekend.

Something had been started that couldn't be stopped, and I had to keep on producing. Next came the Easter work "No Greater Love." Like "Night of Miracles" it was completely original. Its popularity, too, was immediate.

Nothing had prepared me for the kind of response these compositions received — and they were *choral* works, the very area where I had always felt least adequate. Only when I saw with my own eyes and heard with my own ears the resounding approval of a large audience did I at last believe myself capable of this kind of work. I crushed one aspect of my inferiority complex underfoot and walked away from it forever.

I should have been on top of the world. The Better Choirs and Singspiration materials with my stamp on them were an undeniable success.

But there was trouble in the "publishing family," and it was becoming more serious.

18

Boca Raton . . . 1975

God of our fathers, whose almighty hand
Leads forth in beauty all the starry band
Of shining worlds in splendor through the skies,
Our grateful songs before Thy Throne arise.

As in some of my early cantatas, a few familiar hymns were used in *I Love America*. Some statements can't be improved upon. Surprises may be added to the arrangement, and the orchestration may give the piece a fresh new sound, but the statement stands in its original grandeur.

A thrill of recognition seems to stir the audience as the first phrase of this majestic old hymn swells forth. And why not? The melody is matchless, the meaning immense.

Refresh Thy people on their toilsome way,
Lead us from night to never-ending day;

Fill all our lives with love and grace divine,
And glory, laud, and praise be ever Thine.

God of our fathers . . . our fathers. . . .

As in a dream I see them marching down the corridors of eternity: pioneers, builders, tillers of the soil, men of faith and courage and stubbornness and hope and an unquenchable trust in God.

The phrase "our fathers" has a poignancy for me, who never really knew my father. Grandfather Nelson, Uncle Harry, my older brothers — how masterfully they played their part, as if at crucial points throughout my life God touched them in various ways to supply my need for authority figures.

Grandfather with his aura of saintliness. Rudy the brilliant musician. Bill, Bob, and Ken, whom I nearly worshiped, and who had such a compelling effect on my spiritual life. Harry, that jolly, earthy farmer, a pal and companion who filled my summers with sunshine.

When I grew to young manhood and went into the armed forces, another uncle, Oscar Nelson, took it upon himself to "adopt" me by correspondence. His timing was uncanny, as if the Holy Spirit nudged him: "Get off a letter to John. He really needs one now." I'd be homesick or discouraged, physically ill in the first stages of flight training, or in despair over my misunderstanding with Marie, and mail call would bring a long, chatty, reassuring letter from Uncle Oscar.

The pattern kept repeating. As a child in the Covenant church I'd had the counsel of Gilbert Otteson. Later other pastors took over as my spiritual guides and confidants. After the war when I got to Moody, older men like George Schuler and Harry Dixon Loes were not only my teachers but also role models and sources of practical advice. Even today, though a grandfather myself, I have a somewhat older friend in Pat Zondervan who, though a partner and colleague, fulfills some of these same functions. Amazing, how the heavenly Father anticipates the needs of His children who commit their lives to

Him! Though my earthly father was taken, the Lord saw to it that I was never fatherless, either in a human or a spiritual sense.

Maybe this accounts for my special feeling toward younger men who work with me. Like Don Wyrtzen, rapt with concentration now at the keyboard as the first section of *I Love America* reaches its climax. When Don first came to me as a young writer, he stirred my fatherly feelings, and at least unconsciously I resolved to do what I could to let his talent develop and come to fruition with whatever help and guidance I could offer.

Perhaps, too, I see in these younger men glimpses of my nephew Don, whom I loved like a brother, whom I was privileged to lead to Christ, and whose life on earth was snuffed out at such an early age. Who can tell?

I glance over the sea of faces in the choir before me and pick out my son-in-law, Candy's husband Rodger Strader, the only member of my family who could be here in Florida tonight. All week long he's been at my beck and call. I didn't intend to make him an errand boy, but it certainly lightened the load, and I'm grateful. Someday Rodger may be on the podium conducting one of my works — or one of his own. If there's anything I can do to help make that happen, the Lord knows I'll try.

If there are years enough left to me on earth to be half the father to my children that they already think I am, to be the kind of grandfather that Grandfather Nelson was to me —

Sorry, Lord. I'm really overreaching, trying to lift the veil of the future. Whatever you have in mind for this mortal flesh will be enough, and more.

Proudly it waves – Old Glory –
Over the land of the free,
Promise of hope and freedom,
Symbol of liberty.

Here it is, the patriotic paean which closes the first part of

I Love America. First a soprano solo with a somewhat florid vocal line — almost the feeling of an oratorio — and Don has built faint echoes of a military band into the orchestration, an intriguing notion that seems to work well. Soon the chorus takes up the theme in broad, sweeping cadences, building, building, building in volume and intensity to the final, wide-open, heart-stopping sound of an F major triad *fortissimo.*

I turn to acknowledge the applause and then sink into my chair, mighty glad for the break, letting the tension ease out of my frame while Torrey Johnson takes up the inevitable business of the offering.

My thoughts wander for a moment, and I'm suddenly brought back by the realization that something unscheduled and peculiar is taking place on stage. A young soldier, carrying a faded, tattered American flag — Who is he? What's going on here?

At the microphone the young man tells a story of rescuing this neglected banner from a flagpole somewhere in town . . . of a squabble with some townspeople that turns into a fracas . . . of arrest and incarceration in the local jail. It's rambling and rather incoherent, and I see Torrey's body go rigid with embarrassment. Try as I might, I can't make sense of this woebegone soldier's tale.

Now he's describing what it's like to spend a few days in jail, and the audience is restive, murmuring. Look here, young fellow, people don't want to hear such tales! I know, because I don't like to disturb myself with thoughts about what goes on behind bars.

When were You in prison, Lord, and we visited You not? Human nature hasn't changed much in two thousand years.

Clearly the young veteran is not fully in command of himself. Is he yet another sorry victim of that incomprehensible war whose effects we'll all have to live with for the rest of our lives? Apparently.

At last the boy allows himself to be diverted, and Torrey redeems the moment somewhat by appealing to our better nature, recalling our pity and understanding of the shattered bodies and disturbed minds always left in the wreckage of war.

But it's a strange discord in the wake of a patriotic celebration. Strange, nerve-jangling. I try to erase this unexpected disturbance from my consciousness and prepare myself for the strenuous task ahead.

Problems, problems! Just when you think your universe is neatly arranged and the Lord is fully in control, that's when Satan chooses to appear, eternally ready to stir up chaos.

19

The chaos that beset Singspiration began not with a gigantic discord, but with disturbing little sour notes that I could never track down. For months I questioned whether the problems were only in my mind, but as the evidence accumulated I knew something real was happening and that it would have to be dealt with openly.

To do this was extremely difficult. I revered Al Smith, almost had him on a pedestal, but when it came to business dealings and discussions of policy, I felt we simply did not communicate.

Material was selling and significant amounts of money were pouring in, but never enough to cover expenses. The Singspiration books continued to be a grand success, and the choir material was going well, too, yet we never saw daylight. The strings that tied together the many programs and projects in which we were involved kept getting more and more snarled.

Soon I faced the fact that the trouble was not confined to our Minneapolis branch, but was in Montrose as well. Al became financially pressed and at last confided in me that bankruptcy was one of his most realistic options.

I could hardly believe it. Here was a man of unusual talents, a far-ranging mind, a brilliant platform personality. As far as our personal relationship was concerned, everything was in order. Al was perfectly square in his dealings with me, never failing in a commitment. It broke my heart to see this great friend facing the possibility of losing the company which had been his life for so many years.

My personal concern, however, was the future of my own music. Most of it was in the Singspiration catalog, and Singspiration was now in jeopardy. I began to get things in writing, which I should have done all along. It was painful, but necessary, to get contractual matters set forth clearly in black and white.

The murkier things became, the more convinced I was that our whole enterprise was going down the tube. At last, in desperation, I put in a call to the Zondervan brothers.

At some earlier point we had considered the possibility of incorporating Singspiration, with Al, Pat Zondervan, Bernie Zondervan, and myself as principal stockholders. Pat and Bernie's business interest in Singspiration consisted of a distributing contract, but their personal interest went far beyond that. They believed in our material. Philosophically and spiritually we saw eye to eye, and I knew they would not want to see Singspiration collapse. In my talk with them I laid it on the line: here was a great company with even greater potential that was about to be wiped out.

Al agreed with me that our situation had deteriorated to the point where a new corporation seemed to be the only solution. We met with the Zondervans and their treasurer, Peter Kladder, talked the whole thing over frankly, and began to lay groundwork for reorganization. All the parties concerned — Bernie, Pat, Al, and I — contributed the assets we had and received stock in return.

The changeover was far from simple. In meeting after

meeting, month after month, we worked on resolving the various values. We met in Washington and several other cities for discussion. At one point we spent an entire day in New York City hammering out details. Finally, after a grueling all-day session in Grand Rapids involving Al and me, Pete, Pat, and Bernie, and their attorneys, we reached an agreement that was satisfactory to everyone.

We were all tired and a bit jittery. Just as we were about to sign the agreement, we encountered one final hurdle. It seemed insurmountable, and because of everyone's exhaustion and edgy nerves, Pat left the meeting, feeling there was no solution. Al seemed shaken, and I felt positively ill. I was convinced that if we didn't sign the agreement that day, we never would, and Singspiration would be lost. In my mind's eye I saw the shadowed figure of a vulture, circling the sky, ready to swoop down and make off with the leavings of a great enterprise.

After some discussion, we followed Pat to his home for one last try. Praise be to God, at nine o'clock we put our signatures on the contract.

The real shocker for me came in a subsequent meeting when Pat said, "I propose that John Peterson be president of Singspiration." This vote of confidence — to which Bernie and Pete acquiesced readily — was a high point in my life. I praised God for the opportunity to take the reins — and better yet, I no longer felt inadequate to the task. Starting years before in my first contract negotiations with Moody Press, I had gotten into a concentrated study of the business angles. During my time with Al I had kept adding to my knowledge and broadening the scope of my expertise. Now I felt I had learned the business, and the fact that these seasoned businessmen recognized this and were willing to trust me to this extent put the coup de grace to my old, tiresome sense of inadequacy in business matters.

Singspiration was secure, and I breathed easier. The choir company, however, continued to have problems and finally was forced to discontinue operations.

But the organization of the company did not solve all

problems, at least as far as Al was concerned. He called me to his house one day and told me with tears in his eyes that continued business pressures made it necessary for him to sell his interest in the corporation. To me it was unthinkable that Al should be out of Singspiration completely. It was his creation! I tried to talk him out of his decision, and he promised to reconsider.

But his situation raised another fear in my mind. At that point Al and I owned 50 percent of the business — although Al's share was larger than mine; the Zondervans held the other 50 percent. If Pat and Bernie bought out Al's stock, where would that leave me? At length I scraped together what money I could and bought some of Al's shares. At this point we each held 25 percent of the stock.

But this move only forestalled what had become inevitable.

The next time Al approached me with a decision to sell out, I could see that it was irrevocable. I no longer tried to change his mind.

Once more we got together with the Zondervans to discuss this new turn of events. The meeting in Grand Rapids was hectic and melancholy, for that day Al seemed broken, defeated. I did not relish the thought of his bowing out of the company. I was so disillusioned at one point that I asked to be bought out as well. The others would not hear of it. If Al and I were both out of the picture, who would run the company?

I protested that there was no way I could acquire further stock. I had tried to borrow money for this purpose and been turned down. Bernie and Pat immediately suggested that they lend me the money themselves and that the three of us become equal partners. To allay any fears I might have, they would assign me 50 percent control of the company for as long as I lived or remained a stockholder.

Convinced that the Lord was leading, I accepted the arrangement, and the agreement was made.

* * *

During the final negotiations with the Zondervans, I reached my fortieth birthday. According to the old saw, life begins at forty. I *was* beginning a new life — as head of a growing company — but whether the business would fulfill its promise under my leadership was anyone's guess. All I could do was try.

And I would try. But beyond that, beyond any limitation of human effort, I realized that I did not have to be unduly concerned about the ultimate impact of my work or my life. Somewhere along the way I had discovered in Scripture a dynamic concept that changed my whole attitude toward endeavor, achievement, and success.

In Ephesians 2:8-10 Paul writes: "For by grace are ye saved through faith; and that not of yourselves: it is the gift of God: not of works, lest any man should boast. For we are his workmanship, created in Christ Jesus unto good works, which God hath before ordained that we should walk in them."

The first part of that passage was meaningful to me when I came to Christ and received the gift of salvation. But it was years later when the significance of the other part of the passage dawned on me.

I took a close look at the verse about good works "which God hath before ordained that we should walk in them." Suddenly it occurred to me that God had works for me planned from all eternity and a path for me to walk that He had long since charted.

In other words, my life was on the drawing boards of heaven before I was born! That thought excited me tremendously. To think that God had a job for me to do, a unique job, and that my responsibility was simply to ascertain what it was! When I grasped the significance of that idea, I realized that God would guide me through whatever He called me to do, no matter how difficult.

It's often said that God's commandments are His enablements, and this signified that He would never give me a job beyond my capabilities. He would provide all that I needed to carry out an assigned task and would never forsake me in any sense, financially or otherwise.

This was a tremendously comforting thing in my life, especially in view of my long history of feeling inadequate. It gave me quietness of heart and poise in the midst of turmoil. Need I tell you that there were moments when I forgot? But when God would bring me to myself again, I would seize on these convictions with a new sense of gratitude. Even when envy stirred up my emotions and I felt threatened by the achievements of "competing" writers, I could be brought back to reality with the realization that I didn't have to compare myself with other people or worry about their success. If others were "getting ahead" of me, that was not my concern. My job was simply to allow God to work in and through me. Nor did I have to worry that anyone else could frustrate God's purpose in my life.

Of course it was my responsibility to keep working to full capacity, because I knew God wanted my best. But the results of my efforts were, in the final analysis, in His control, and His responsibility.

* * *

Shortly before Al left the company, I was able to hire Norman Johnson as a full-time associate. In 1960 we had acquired the part-time service of Norm, a long-time friend of mine. Our association went back to 1950 when he had written to me as a student at North Park College, introducing himself as a product of Lindsborg, Kansas, where his family had been well acquainted with mine. Norm had sent me two additional stanzas to my chorus "I Surrender All," and I liked what he had written; in subsequent editions his stanzas were included. He was well-trained, with a master's degree from Southern California University at the time he joined our staff, and had worked for us out of an office on the West Coast. Then in January, 1962 he and his family left their Southern California home and joined us in Montrose.

With Al gone there didn't seem to be any compelling

reason for us to maintain our offices in Montrose. Therefore, the Norm Johnsons and the John Petersons laid plans to move to Grand Rapids where we could be close to the Zondervan Publishing House. I rehired Harold DeCou, who had been living in Wheaton, Illinois, working for Youth for Christ, and he and his family also made arrangements to move to Michigan.

We sold our house in January of 1963 and moved into an apartment while a house was being built for us in Grand Rapids. What a lot of happiness we had experienced as a family in that old green-shuttered building! The girls had done most of their growing up there; Sandi, the oldest, was a young woman now, and Pam, the youngest, about to enter the teenage years.

They were wonderful children — quick, affectionate, full of surprises — and they loved music! All three had studied piano, and at an early age they started to sing together, not at the urging of their fond parents, strangely enough, but on their own initiative. We were thrilled to think that the Lord had given them talent and that they were willing to use it for Him. Marie and I encouraged them in their singing, trying not to be pushy about it, and whenever they were invited to perform in some church we were happy to give our consent.

The girls also began to make an impact on my writing. They listened patiently and critically to my new works, often offering good suggestions for changes. With youngsters of my own, I made more of an effort to keep in touch with the tastes and preferences of their age group. People find "youth-oriented" rhythms and harmonies in some of my later works, and perhaps this is the reason.

My compositions were finding an ever-widening audience. There were translations into Arabic, Portuguese, Korean, Chinese, Polish, Swedish, Spanish, French, and German. Even more surprising to me was their acceptance beyond the evangelical family. Reports kept coming in of their use by Mormon, liberal, and Roman Catholic churches. The worldwide audience I had dreamed of was now mine, not only through individual songs, but through larger choral works. This gave me far greater satisfaction than I would have received from simply having an occasional "hit."

20

Boca Raton . . . 1975

We're into the second half of the musical now. The patriotism section is over (I hope it wasn't too much; goodness knows we wrung it out to the last drop.), and we're getting to the crux of the matter.

The soprano voices rise in a descant over the main theme — "Praise the Lord and give thanks, America" — in a counter-melody which is Pam's creation. She stood by the piano as I worked one day and improvised a vocal line which I immediately penciled into the manuscript. Praise the Lord and give thanks for Pam, too.

I wish they all could have been here tonight; Marie and the girls and Tom, my other son-in-law. I know they're here in spirit, but their physical presence would be an added blessing. If ever a man had a family who made him feel like king of the hill, I'm that man. Yet they know me better than anyone else — know my faults and sins and weak spots — see the warts and blemishes that never appear on the glossy image I show the world. And still they always give me the feeling, somehow, that I can do no wrong.

Here's one of the paradoxes of the Christian life: the more you accept God's grace to be open, honest, and fallible with your family; the more you include them in your problems; the more you let your wife and children see your dependence on the Lord — the more He makes you loved and even a bit heroic in their eyes.

I don't understand it, but I praise Him for this mysterious design.

From the time our girls were able to talk, Marie and I openly shared our dilemmas with them, included them in our plans and prayers. More fully than anyone else on earth they know how often I have to cry out to God for help and direction, how often I knock at the door of 1 John 1:9 to seek forgiveness and cleansing.

Rather than diminishing me in their eyes, this seems to make it possible for them to express their own needs and failings. Very little is hid from one another in our family, and yet — that divine paradox again — with each dark fear and murky problem laid on the altar of God for His solution, the family bonds seem to grow stronger; the light of mutual trust and love grows brighter.

God has given me this relationship with my family. Where would I be without it? The stoicism and reticence of my Swedish forebears is very strong in my nature. In the other relationships of my life — even with the closest, most trusted friends and colleagues — I have always found it painfully difficult to speak about my weaknesses and needs.

The volatility of my artistic temperament has been masked by a cool calm which, I suppose, looks like self-sufficiency or even egotism. (At least, I *think* it's been masked. Perhaps people know me better than I guess — have a more accurate reading on me than I am willing to admit.)

A few years ago I was being torn apart by anxiety over my

physical health. Annoying allergic episodes were turning into occasional agonizing traumas, and no amount of prayer or medical attention seemed to have any effect. At Singspiration I had an enormous work load and never-ending responsibilities. My partners and associates were partly aware of my difficulty, but I found it difficult to talk with them about the extent of my discomfort.

It seemed important to keep the momentum going at all costs and not burden my associates with a situation they couldn't alleviate. They had their own problems and responsibilities. It appeared to me that to involve them in my health difficulties would be selfish, so I kept the whole thing pretty much in the family.

One afternoon when the burden of business had been especially heavy, Pat Zondervan called and suggested I join him and a couple of other fellows on the golf course for some much-needed exercise and recreation. In the middle of the game I felt an attack coming on, a bad one. Within minutes, I knew, I would be fighting for breath and desperately in need of medical help.

Even under those conditions I struggled to maintain my composure and not let Pat and the others see what was happening. I excused myself and painfully made my way back to the club house with the help of a caretaker. Not a moment too soon. A delivery man who happened to be on the scene took one look at me and telephoned my wife. When Marie arrived a few minutes later, the two of them helped me into the car and we speeded off for medical attention. There was no mistaking the fear in Marie's eyes, though she remained calm and controlled.

Only much later did I finally tell Pat the whole truth about that day on the golf course. My Swedish reticence! Sometimes I wonder if it's a blessing or a curse. What a strange and wondrous creature is man — what a mélange of emotions and inhibitions. Within myself I've always been aware of paradoxical qualities: spiritual and romantic impulses that could give birth to a lush, soaring melody — and then the cool secretiveness that kept problems hidden from the world.

Except from my family. They are my safety valve. With them there's no need to be anyone more or less than myself.

I have no secrets from Marie. She knows me inside and out and loves me despite everything — as I have loved her always, devotedly and exclusively. Moreover, she has the ability to rejoice and to suffer with me in a bond of absolute trust and confidentiality. I can share anything with her with the knowledge that it will never reach someone else's ears. If ever there was a woman who lived up to the biblical concept of the wife as her husband's helpmeet, it's Marie.

21

As the new president of a corporation in a new location, with a thousand knots to unravel, I needed every bit of support, encouragement, and understanding I could get from my wife and children. And they never failed to provide it.

We had been through "tight" times together. There had been a lot of "making do." Now, on the surface at least, our position had improved greatly. We lived in a beautiful home, had a variety of good food on the table and a new car in the driveway, and our wardrobe was a far cry from those days when Marie wore hand-me-downs while I grew progressively shabbier. The Lord, for reasons of His own, had faithfully seen us through from poverty to the comforts of the middle class. The concerns I brought to His throne were now far more complex and unnerving than new shoes for the baby or last month's electric bill.

Within the family I had a priceless resource in our devotional life, and I never had to seek God's wisdom alone. To be sure, when I was convicted of sin I stood before Him naked and solitary, but with policy decisions, confusing options, and issues affecting our family life, Marie stood with me as a full prayer partner, and the girls were included almost as completely.

I had been taught that it was important to maintain a strong Christian influence in the home and to establish a daily time of family devotions. Marie believed this as strongly as I did, and despite some unavoidable gaps we always tried to maintain consistent family worship.

How I pity those who have never discovered the riches that are ours when we come together as families to pray, share our concerns, air our grievances, express our needs, and, above all, learn what it means to rest on the unshakeable promises of God! His promises were never meant to tease us — to be nothing but pious, idle chatter. They were given so that we might test them and find them reliable. Why face life's crises and battles alone when God wants to be on your side? It's all so wasteful and unnecessary.

For that matter, why cheat yourself of the unspeakable joy of seeing your children opening up to God's wisdom and guidance? Of course there are times when you must go "into a closet" alone. But there are a hundred thousand other opportunities to let your children hear you pray aloud, to know that dad and mother are as much in need of grace as anyone else.

Because we never hid our needs from the girls, because this attitude was as much a part of our life as eating breakfast, they felt free to be open about their own concerns and cares. Nothing was too unimportant to become a matter for prayer. To family devotions they brought whatever was on their minds: school tests and projects, programs they were involved in, conflicts with their playmates.

We also prayed regularly for various Christian workers, and though they might not know them personally, the girls became attached to certain preachers and missionaries who were "theirs" in a special way. When she was hardly more than a baby, Candy prayed earnestly for "the missionaries in the cornfield" — her garbled version of "missionaries in the foreign field" — but we did not laugh, and she continued in sincere faith.

It was important to us as parents to instill in our children a God-consciousness and the fact that we were living for Him, obligated to Him, and on His eternal business. They all seemed to grasp this, and eventually, as they matured, each one in turn committed her life to Christ.

When they reached their teen-age years, we had the usual concerns of all nuclear-age parents. Young people of today have to face things we never dreamed of! But we tried to fortify them spiritually with consistent Christian living, prayer and Bible teaching in the home, Sunday school and church, and a round of activity in Christian youth groups. Despite all this fortification, there were times when Marie and I fussed and fumed a bit — about certain friendships the girls made, about situations that arose, about conditions and temptations among their contemporaries. Thank the Lord, all three remained true to their commitment to Him.

The moral, emotional, and spiritual support I got from Marie and the girls during my early days as president of Singspiration can never be measured. My staff, too, were an asset on which I could put no price in human terms. And my new partners, Bernie and Pat Zondervan, were showing me a way of doing business as Christians which was a revelation.

I was terrifically impressed with the spiritual dimension of their business life. To be involved with men whose one goal was to make Christ known to the world was an immense experience. It felt so solid. If a decision was made to do something, I could be sure *that something* would be done. Here were men of integrity and rectitude who stood by their word and wouldn't let anyone down.

Though not a musician himself, Pat's enthusiasm for my compositions never flagged. He loved music and had the remarkable ability of sending a word of cheer just when I needed it most. Like the time he wrote me from London where he had attended a meeting during Billy Graham's London Crusade: "Cliff (Barrows) is using 'Surely Goodness and Mercy' each night. He says he gets notes sent up to the platform if he doesn't use it early in the service."

The Zondervans' teamwork was almost uncanny, though they were unique individuals: Pat, the man of action and decisiveness, the trailblazer; Bernie, a bit more quiet, with a somewhat visionary spiritual quality. True to their word, they never tried to call the tune when it came to artistic policy. I had the staff I wanted, even a building separate from the main publishing house. I set my own pace and operated in my own way. We counseled together at least once a month, and they made valuable suggestions, but basically the creative and production sides of Singspiration were in my hands.

I had been warned not to move to Grand Rapids — warned that I'd get caught up in a business routine and my creative juices would dry up. If anything, the opposite happened. Pat, especially, had the "go get 'em" quality that a person of my temperament needed to push me ahead. He and Bernie also had wisdom on another count. They knew that if I were to create, I had to have a certain amount of isolation. They gave me that, along with a show of confidence that was beyond anything I had known before.

We were, however, running into a messy situation which had nothing to do with our relationship, but which cut severely into my time for writing and composing. It was a situation that had to be resolved, and I was the only person who could logically do it.

One of my first duties was to get all our copyrights in order, and as I began going through the files I soon realized that this would be a herculean task. Carelessness in acquiring material and nailing down copyrights over a period of many years had resulted in a tangle of colossal dimensions. I'd spend hours combing through files, poring over records and come up with my head swimming. What belonged to us and what didn't? Sometimes it was impossible to determine.

I must have spent two years straightening out the mess. I went personally to many composers, getting their signatures on contracts. By painful degrees we extricated ourselves from the snarl, the Zondervans trusting me to handle most of it because of my knowledge of copyright matters.

With those mares' nests finally cleared away, I could concentrate on two other goals I had set for the company: first, a high standard of excellence in publication — accuracy and the best writing and arranging we could produce. Second, I was concerned that our publications squared with Scripture. As a writer I had always felt that the Lord would hold me accountable for the message conveyed in my songs, and if the lyrics waffled on biblical truth, they would not meet acceptable standards. My partners concurred. The cornerstone of their publishing company was the Bible as the inspired, inerrant, authoritative Word of God.

By these strict standards a lot of material in the old Singspiration catalog had to be discarded — some nice tunes, but with lyrics that didn't measure up to the goal we had set. My assistants, Norm Johnson and Harold DeCou, both top-notch musicians and dedicated Christians, shared my determination to achieve excellence in both music and lyrics. And, of course, the more we wrote and edited, the more we learned. Soon the company's reputation was enhanced. Our customers and our competitors looked at us with new respect, respect which showed up in an unprecedented acceptance of our material. My cantatas alone had now achieved sales in the millions, and people were clamoring for more.

I began to put more time and effort into writing full-length works, and they were coming forth at one or two a year: *Behold Your King*, *The Glory of Easter*, *Born a King*, *The Sound of Singing*, and on and on. At times I was under tremendous pressure to complete a project with a deadline hanging over my head.

But this was nothing new. Back in Montrose, for example, when I was trying to finish *No Greater Love* and was overdue, I had to get the manuscript in the mail on a Saturday afternoon or it would not reach Norm Johnson on the West Coast in time to be checked over and taken to the plate man to have engravings made.

Saturday arrived, and I was still working on the final pages of the last chorus. The post office would close at five o'clock; I was feeling pretty harried. At the last possible moment I stuffed the manuscript into an envelope, jumped into the car, and drove to the post office.

After I got home, I wrote Norm a note: "Just a few minutes ago I mailed the cantata. . . . I am counting on you to go over the manuscript very carefully to spot any mistakes or omissions I may have made in my haste. By the way, in the excitement to get the thing mailed, I failed to put on my brake when parking in front of the post office. As a result, my car rolled half a block down the wrong side of the street and finally wrapped itself around a telephone pole!"

The pressure to keep producing was healthy enough, but occasionally I would regret that I had rushed a work to completion when I looked back later and found something that could have been improved. There's leisure in hindsight, of course, but a bit more leisure might have avoided some of the necessity for hindsight.

Usually when I finished something, however, I had the ability to let it go and say, "That's it." I had no choice, for I was always faced with another immediate commitment — or there were half-finished works that demanded attention. Having completed a composition, I could never afford the luxury of dwelling on a sense of achievement. I had to let it go and press on.

* * *

Choral clinics and workshops became an important part of my work during the 1960s. With increasing frequency I traveled around the country to meet and work with the thousands of choir directors who used Singspiration music. Conducting performances of my works also began to take a heavy toll on my time and strength, though this was something that gave me pleasure.

How much poorer I would be to have missed the opportunity to conduct *No Greater Love* in Philadelphia's Convention Hall, with 500 singers and a dramatic cast and over 11,000 in the audience. Or to lead 1,200 exuberant young people in singing *The Good Life* before an audience of 25,000 in the Cincinnati Reds' ball park. Or to guide 50 untrained but enthusiastic voices through a rendition of *So Send I You* in Soldotna, Alaska.

During the summers I always managed to get away for a brief time with my family. Marie and I had made a point of vacationing with the children all through the years, even when we were financially strapped. Those times with the family were periods of renewal and refreshment which I needed desperately.

When the girls began to go off to college, it sometimes seemed to Marie and me that we were rattling around in an empty house, although we should have been glad of the opportunity to "rattle," for my trips away were becoming more frequent, and I usually traveled alone, with Marie staying at home.

At the time of her graduation from high school, Sandi seemed to be in a period of uncertainty, but she was a Christian and anxious to do the Lord's will. At last she decided to go to Moody Bible Institute. Her year there made a great impact. She matured spiritually and gained a deeper understanding of the Word of God. She also benefited by the association with young people who felt the pull of God on their lives and were choosing to prepare for Christian service.

Following her year at Moody, she transferred to a junior college in Grand Rapids and then completed her college work at Western Michigan University in Kalamazoo. Candy also attended Moody for a brief period and then the Baptist Bible College in Grand Rapids.

Pam — to leap forward in time — began her higher

education at Trinity College and was graduated from the Grand Rapids School of the Bible and Music, later doing further academic work at Grand Canyon College.

The three of them worked hard at their singing, and the sound they produced as a trio became more polished. The first of their several record albums was cut in the early sixties, sparking a career that later would include a fairly regular spot on the "Day of Discovery" telecast and a tour of Sweden — a fabulous adventure and an opportunity for them to give their Christian witness.

* * *

Bernie Zondervan, my treasured friend and colleague, died in 1966.

Pat took the death of his brother heroically, in the spirit of the Resurrection, but it was a terrible loss. They were spiritual brothers as well as blood brothers — Pat having led Bernie to Christ only a day after he himself had committed his life to the Lord as a young man — and they had worked together in a comfortable double harness for many, many years.

Then, just three years later, death took Bernie, Jr., a true "chip off the old block," who had been groomed to take his father's place in the business. Sad days, tempered only by the assurance of the Lord; victory over death and the promise of eternal life to come.

The weight of my responsibilities increased steadily, augmented by travel and outside conducting duties. And I kept adding "extracurricular" activities, which may have been ill-considered but which brought a refreshing change from the publishing business and enriched my life with new friends and associations. In 1967 I was named to the boards of both Gospel Films and the Grand Rapids School of the Bible and Music. Billy Zeoli of Gospel Films and John Miles of the school were soon numbered among my most valued friends.

Serving on the film board intrigued me. Soon I became involved in the making of a musical film, *Worlds Apart,* writing songs for it and generally assisting in the production. It was a change of pace I was grateful to have — especially later when it became obvious that scores of people were coming to Christ through seeing this film and responding to its gospel message.

My work load was indeed heavy, but I never considered it onerous. I had so far overcome my early diffidence and insecurity in business matters that I now felt fully capable of running the corporation.

Still I realized that overwork would not benefit either me or the company, so to ease my load we recruited some outstanding people to join the staff. Norm Johnson and Harold DeCou were still my capable right-hand men. Jack Rasley, who had been with the Lorenz Company, added further strength to the team. And finally Don Wyrtzen was brought in as head of our youth division.

As the new staff meshed and duties were reassigned, I was satisfied that we had made a good move and relaxed somewhat. But business was booming, and everyone's work load multiplied. Adding to the pressure I personally felt as the 1960s raced by was the disconcerting change in my physical condition: an irritating allergic condition that grew worse instead of better. I had the usual tests and desensitizing shots but found only slight relief.

All my life I had enjoyed perfect health. My morbid fantasies during childhood about being a candidate for early death were no more than the products of a vivid imagination. But now my nose dripped constantly, and I was running to doctors here and there in search of relief — even a futile trip to a "super" doctor in the Southwest who, well-meaning friends assured me, had the answer to everything.

Polyps were found in my nose, and I seized on this discovery as the probable cause of my misery. After the polyps were removed surgically, I did feel better for several months, but then the allergic episodes returned, accompanied now by symptoms of asthma. I didn't really know what asthma was, and frankly, I was scared.

I learned that asthma was regarded frequently by many medical experts as a psychogenic disease tied to psychological pressures and tension. Should I continue to be involved with the administration of the business? Should I devote my time to writing? Should I stop traveling? Above all, what was the Lord trying to show me?

What began as a minor annoyance had become a battle raging in my heart.

22

Boca Raton . . .1975

It's time to pray to the God who watches o'er us;
It's time to seek His help without delay.

Here we are back in familiar John Peterson territory: a gospel-type song. My good friend Steve Boalt is singing, and the audience is hushed, as if straining to catch every word.

The world is dark, for the clouds of war still threaten;
It's time for all America to pray!
If we would keep the flag of freedom flying,
Secure the peace for which we all are crying,
It's time to pray, our sin and wrong confessing,
It's time for all America to pray!

I believe this with all my heart. There is none guiltless among us — "none righteous; no, not one." Those of us who have loved and served the Lord for decades are as much in need of grace and forgiveness as the most wayward, unthinking soul. All of us share our national guilt. If my song can convey this in some small way, can persuade a few Americans to find their way back to an attitude of prayer. . . .

What a sad day it will be if, in the church, we ever become too sophisticated for such songs or for genuine gospel songs! They are truly "heart music," for their simplicity and directness have a way of speaking to the most basic needs of man.

Not to everyone, of course. Engraved on my memory is the letter of stinging rebuke someone wrote about me years ago in *Christianity Today:*

> Do you not realize that Mr. Peterson has done as much as anyone in the last decade to degrade church music? What once was our glorious musical heritage has been so prostituted as to give us in its stead a frivolous, worldly, and spiritually corrupting corpus of song, which uplifts no one, certainly entertains many, and is completely incapable of inducing worship.

Prostituted . . . frivolous . . . corrupting. . . . And here I'd been seeing myself as part of a great line of sacred composers and musicians who had served God, enriched the world, and brought joy to the hearts of men. Well, well — I'd be a fool indeed if I expected everyone to love me.

And I can't be too upset by the criticism of individuals when I look around and realize that sacred music has a greater appeal today than ever before, to Christians and even to non-Christians. Moreover, there is little need any more to water down the message of a gospel song for the so-called secular world. The name of Jesus is spoken, and sung, loud and clear. Even in pop songs we find references to the blood of the cross, without the same offense, it seems, as back when I wrote "Over the Sunset Mountains" and a nervous publisher asked me to replace the name of Jesus with a more "acceptable" reference to heaven.

With the widespread resurgence of interest in spiritual things, particularly among young people, gospel songs have come into their own in a way undreamed of two decades ago. A few years back when Tennessee Ernie Ford was cutting some gospel albums, a producer at Capitol Records told me those albums were selling better than anything else Capitol had produced. Sacred music has become big business.

There are a couple of ways to look at this fascinating development. It can be a problem or a blessing. Some of my more conservative Christian friends find it dangerous that our music has gotten outside the church and into secular society. Commercialization and exploitation are certainly realities, and I share this concern. But I can't let it thwart me from pursuing my calling. Despite the intense commercialism of some of the gospel music business, I believe that the inherent message is coming through, and I trust God to use it as He will.

I find it difficult to imagine anyone listening to Don Wyrtzen's song which the choir is now singing and finding it "commercial." There's heartfelt sincerity here.

When we walk before the Lord in faithfulness each day,
When we bow before His Word, His statutes to obey,
He promises to hear, He promises to heal,
And He promises to bless and to forgive.

If my people, who are called by my name, shall humble
themselves and pray,
And seek my face and turn from their wicked ways,
Then will I hear from heaven, and will forgive their sin,
And will heal their land.

He will hear; He will heal.

23

He will heal?

For many months I bombarded heaven with prayers for deliverance from my physical ailments, but healing eluded me. My family knew what I was suffering, but I did not speak of my problems to anyone on the staff at Singspiration. Meanwhile, I went from doctor to doctor, trying just about everything but acupuncture. And I kept trying to put a good face on things. About a month after the terrifying attack on the golf course I wrote in a round-robin letter to my far-flung family:

"Believe me, I had some bad times during the past few months. I am on a steady diet of pills to keep the allergies in check. . . . However, if I am careful, and with proper medication, I will probably be okay. Right now I feel fine. The doctor has put me through a series of tests, not so much that he expected anything to be wrong, but to put my own fears to rest. I am going to try to avoid, as much as possible, tension-producing meetings and situations. . . ."

Attempting to discount my difficulties, I went on accepting invitations. A good friend, Sumner Wemp, had become president of Southeastern Baptist College in Birmingham, and when I was asked to go there to conduct a choral workshop and direct a performance of my cantata *So Send I You* I could not resist.

A missions conference was in progress at the school, and I arrived a day early to take part in it. By noon on the day I was to conduct the workshop I had developed a severe headache and had taken some aspirin. I felt ill, but did not want to disappoint the choir directors who were there for the workshop, so I set my jaw and launched into it.

I got through the first anthem, then suddenly felt an awful constricting sensation in my chest. It was unlike anything I had experienced before. I realized I was in real trouble. In the audience was a choir director whom I knew quite well; I signaled him to take over the workshop and then stumbled out of the building. By the time I got outside — Mrs. Wemp following to see what was wrong — I was just able to gasp for air.

A medical doctor who happened to be at the school that day, the husband of one of the alumnae who had gathered for the occasion, saw my plight, got a car, and rushed me to a hospital. That is, Sumner drove the car with me beside him and the doctor in the back seat. I leaned out the window, fighting for air, barely managing to get out the words, "I don't think I'm going to make it."

It was a hideous sensation. I was certain I was dying, and along with the many thoughts that raced through my mind was a bit of puzzlement: *Lord,* I thought, *how strange that You brought me all the way to Birmingham to take me home!*

In the hospital emergency room I was given oxygen, and a chest x-ray and electrocardiogram were taken at once. To me it all seemed rather pointless, for I was sure I would soon be gone. Nurses came in to ask for the names and addresses of my next of kin — a hospital routine, but in my mind another indication that death was imminent. I had perfect peace and no fear for myself, but I thought about my family and how terribly shocked they would be.

After a time the shots and pills the doctors had given me began to have some effect. There was a breaking sensation in my chest, and I was able to breathe easier.

Toward evening, Sumner came in and asked how I was feeling. "A little better," I said. About five hours had now passed and the thought of death was receding. I supposed that I had had a heart attack. Sumner said no, the tests showed no damage to my heart.

The doctor who had helped rush me to the hospital had not left my side during those hours, and he remained with me through most of the evening until it was clear that my condition was not critical and that I was, in fact, improving.

When the hospital doctors were filled in on my past history, they theorized that I had had a severe allergic reaction, probably to the aspirin I had taken that morning.

The following day, still very weak, I was able to go on to St. Petersburg where a concert was scheduled in one of the large Methodist churches. I was even able to conduct the second half of the concert.

The experience really shook me. True, I was not afraid to die if it was God's will. But if I had some years left on earth, I wanted to be able to make the most of them, and I was now convinced that my work load was aggravating my physical problems.

There were invitations, however, that I could not refuse. Shortly after the Birmingham incident I went to Alaska for some concerts and a series of workshops and had trouble all the time I was there. Before the first concert, on a Sunday afternoon with the high school auditorium full and a massed choir on stage, I had another attack. *Why, Lord? Why not wait at least till after the concert?* There had been no aspirin this time; it was a plain asthma attack.

Fortunately I happened to be staying in the home of a doctor who hurried to his clinic and got me a shot of adrenalin.

The concert was delayed half an hour, the choir praying for me. Somewhat recovered, I found enough strength to go on and conduct, using one hand.

Throughout the rest of the Alaska tour I tottered on the edge of another spasm, but managed to keep going. En route home I changed planes in Seattle and got onto a huge plane full of servicemen returning from Vietnam. Every seat was filled, and the passenger section was blue with cigarette smoke. Within minutes after takeoff I was leaning forward in my seat, gasping, trying to stay alive. The torment of not being able to get one satisfying breath was nearly unbearable. At last we reached O'Hare airport in Chicago, and as I waited in the lobby for my plane to Grand Rapids, I finally made a partial recovery.

I was hesitant to level with Pat Zondervan and Pete Kladder, who was now president of Zondervan. Hesitant, because I didn't want to undermine anyone's confidence in my ability to run things. Singspiration was strong and growing. Vigorous leadership was essential.

I recognized, too, that I had fallen in love with the business end of things, even while it crowded me. It was invigorating, satisfying, and God was leading. I couldn't picture myself out of my position of authority.

But the illness was tearing me apart. It wasn't constant, but would hit me periodically. All the while I kept worrying about my staff and their families, becoming more emotionally involved than an executive should. I felt a strong burden for them.

Pat knew we were planning a winter vacation in Phoenix. After learning more about my physical problems, he suggested I spend several months there — thinking perhaps the dry air and sunshine might do me good. It was impossible for me to get away for so long a time, but Marie and I did spend two weeks in the "Valley of the Sun" and were immediately enchanted with it. The atmosphere was pleasant, the natural beauty of the place was breathtaking, and I did feel better. We toyed with the idea of establishing a winter headquarters there, thus getting away from Michigan's damp cold. It just might work: I could keep in close touch with the office by phone, and when the worst of the winter was over we could return to Grand Rapids. Our children were grown and didn't need us around at all times to ride herd on them. The more we tossed the idea around, the more reasonable it seemed.

* * *

Coincidentally, another development was taking place over which I had no control and which put me in the position of having to make a drastic decision about my future. The Zondervan Publishing House was about to undergo a major reorganization. Business had been tremendous, the Lord was blessing in an unusual way, and Pat and his associates had some dreams for further expansion. To accomplish these plans they would need additional capital, and the only way to raise it was to go public with the corporation.

This move would obviously have an effect on Singspiration. Those of us in management began to talk and pray about what it might mean with reference to our company. In 1969 we had initiated a profit-sharing plan which raised the morale of the staff and made everyone feel he had more of a stake in the business. All of us had a proprietary feeling about Singspiration — I more than anyone. With the reorganization of the parent company, would Singspiration get swallowed up? And where did we all fit into the picture?

Another crucial question began to dominate my waking thoughts and even interrupt my sleep. Where did God's blessing rest on me most heavily? I had to admit that it was in the creative area. A good executive could be hired to replace me in my administrative duties, but a creative talent was the product of years of nurture. And I could not ignore my illness — it hovered over me like a vicious bird of prey, ready to strike at any moment.

I laid the whole issue before Marie and the girls, and we

prayed about it for months, for whatever I did would affect their future as well as mine. The idea of stepping down as president of Singspiration was painful. For ten years I had run the company and found enormous satisfaction in doing so. Even as I discussed with my staff the possibility of selling out Singspiration to the new Zondervan Corporation and letting the new organization absorb the old, I clung to my job like a frightened mother bear clinging to her cub.

One morning I found myself picking up the phone and calling Pat. Without thinking I blurted, "Why don't you buy me out?" It was impulsive — I could not have been serious. But I said it.

That suggestion, bursting out of months of pressure and prayer and discussion, set wheels turning. Once the issue was out in the open, we could deal with it.

We worked out an agreement whereby all of us would sell our stock in Singspiration. I would give up my administrative responsibilities and be free to use my time in writing and traveling. It took months of negotiation to thresh out the details of the new arrangement, but all through the process it seemed that God was putting the pattern together beautifully. On February 2, 1971, the agreements were signed.

It was a bittersweet moment — there was the relief of knowing that I had been obedient to God's leading, but sadness that my departure would break up a team which had become marvelously close-knit over the years. When I had first told Norm and Harold of my decision, we had all been close to tears. But now it was done, and I comforted myself with the thought that the new arrangement would be beneficial to them, opening up new areas for their development and growth.

Giving up the presidency would not mean severing relations with the company or going into retirement. But I would no longer be in a key post. There would be no secretaries at my beck and call, no people waiting on me for direction. The hectic excitement of the office would go on without me.

I went home with an awful, sinking feeling in my heart.

* * *

Marie and I decided that a clean break from Grand Rapids would be advisable. Moreover, it would allow us to pursue the dream of a permanent home in Arizona. We had explored the area around Phoenix and had fallen in love with the little town of Carefree just north of the city. Accordingly, we bought a plot of land on the side of Black Mountain and hired a local man to design a home for us. His sketches struck us as tasteful and imaginative — a low-lying building that would follow the contours of the terrain and blend harmoniously into the desert vegetation.

Our imminent departure from Michigan initiated a rush of activity among friends and colleagues and temporarily cushioned the emotional shock of my no longer being at my desk. Calvary Church, where we had our membership and where I had served for years as music director and song leader, regaled us with several farewell functions, including a banquet and a concert of my music. The Grand Rapids School of the Bible and Music honored me with the presentation of a framed inscription recalling my writing career and my long association with the school as board member and chairman of the board and also by naming their newly acquired music facility the "John W. Peterson Music Building."

While Marie oversaw the packing and shipping of our furniture and household effects, I tore into the vast accumulation of personal records and correspondence that would have to be moved to our new home in Carefree. As I thumbed through a mountain of papers, some of them now yellow with age, I was overwhelmed with the sheer weight of the evidence of what my music had meant to people. In every part of the world, it seemed, were those who had found in my material precisely what I wanted it to convey.

Here was a handwritten letter from a woman who had found in the words of my little chorus "He Owns the Cattle on a

Thousand Hills" the courage to commit to God an awful (and justified) resentment, and the strength to go on to a new life in His grace. And here was a note from one of my nephews, a missionary in Brazil, telling me that the song "Heaven Came Down and Glory Filled My Soul" had become so popular in his corner of the world that "even the monkeys are singing it!" Here were treasured mementos of friends long since gone to glory — newspaper clippings — flattering reviews of my cantatas — fan mail — warm personal greetings from giants in the field of sacred music — and much, much more. As I pondered it over, nearly numb with emotion, I thought, *O Lord, how much love can one sinner absorb in his lifetime?* And, *Thank You, Lord. Thank You.*

24

Boca Raton . . . 1975

Jesus is calling America – calling her back to the fold.
Jesus is calling America – calling the young and the old.
Back to the "faith of our fathers," faith we need in these
troubled days –

It's nearly over. This softly urgent call to repentance, then a final blazing chorus of "The Battle Hymn of the Republic," and I can turn over the last page of my conducting score and sit down.

Torrey will lead the people in prayer, in his own persuasive way asking for decisions from those in the audience who have not yet yielded their lives to Christ and exhorting the faithful to a renewal of their commitment. But my part will be finished. I'll be able to bend my head and heart in prayer and commit this evening to whatever use the Lord wants to make of it. Then there will be greetings, handshakes, thanks to the performers, time to unwind, and finally sleep. Tomorrow holds a new challenge, and today will be a memory.

I Love America will pass from my hands into those whose responsibility it is to print and distribute it, and into the libraries of choir directors and singers all over the nation. In a sense it will pass into history, for it will belong to the world.

I'm glad none of that is my responsibility — that I can trust others to do their jobs as they trust me to do mine. Something about the selling and distribution of my work has always been a thorn in my flesh. I know how vital it is, but I've been sensitive to the criticism of people outside the field who regard gospel songwriters as a bunch of hucksters; people who see our work as nothing more than merchandise to be peddled like the latest model from General Motors.

Yes, I'm sensitive to this charge, though I know in my heart that such critics don't really grasp what we are all about. They can't accept the fact that what motivates us is to glorify Christ, not to sell Him.

No one is more aware than I of the need to get our work out into the world, to use the framework of promotion and distribution channels. I recognize the fact that the more we sell, the wider will be our ministry. If the sharp jibes of cynics still hit the mark, it's because I have tussled with the problem all my life, not because I don't trust God to have His way. Long ago I got it settled in my mind that my aim was not to make money by selling Jesus or "promoting" the gospel, but to lift Him up. Through periods of privation and prosperity I have sought to do exactly the same thing: to serve Him. This was my calling and, in need or in luxury, my only significant reward.

In all honesty I can say that even when I was literally hungry, I never regretted my decision to live for God, nor did I resent being poor by worldly standards. And when my work gained widespread acceptance and God lavished earthly gifts on me and my loved ones, my attitude remained unchanged. I enjoy the comforts money can buy; I don't deny it. But I like to believe that — like Job of old — even if all this were taken from me, I would serve and love and trust God still.

These deep things in my soul — I wonder if I will ever reach the point where I can share them openly with other Christians, or whether I will always have to express my most meaningful emotions in terms of lyrics and music. I've had a problem with openness in fellowship; I'm the kind of guy who holds everything inside. I can take my burdens to the Lord and leave them there. But with people? Only Marie. A couple of weeks ago I was so uptight I almost flew apart, wracked with tension over this conference and some other duties which crowded in on me. At last the floodgates burst, and for about an hour I ranted while Marie listened. Once it was out in the open, I felt better. If Marie hadn't been there, I don't know what I would have done.

But maybe even my insularity has been useful to God. It could be that my inability to be open and forthright about problems and needs, resulting in my having to express them in song, has been part of His plan for my life. That's an intriguing thought! God doesn't let anything go to waste. A creative person always uses his experiences as grist to the mill in his work. The Lord allows disappointments and trials, as He does to all people, and inevitably the artist incorporates them into his compositions. Having been through the fire and found victory by the grace of God, he has something to say which he would not have had if he had lived a serene, untroubled life.

An intriguing thought — and it leads to others.

Suppose, for example, the Lord never answered my prayers for healing precisely because it took something that drastic to shake me loose from my beloved administrative work. Suppose He wanted me to be free to create, to apply myself more fully to the area of writing where His blessing had been so evident.

Without my illness, it could not have happened. Of course, of course! It's all so obvious, and it never occurred to me until this moment. *My pleas for healing could not be answered just then:* they ran counter to God's will for my life.

Well, then, *Thank You, Lord, for every bit of anguish and uncertainty. Thank You for getting me out of that comfortable rut and back into the mainstream of Your purpose. Thank You, Lord, thank You.*

Nothing goes to waste.

25

Paeans of congratulation were still ringing in my ears when Marie and I got to our new home in Arizona, and I sank into the worst depression I had ever known.

No one will ever comprehend how difficult it was. Though I intended to go on producing as much as before, I suffered all the withdrawal symptoms that a person goes through who shuts the door on his work life forever. Unthinking friends would josh me about my "retirement" (At your age?), and the knife would twist. My fantasies of lazy afternoons on the golf course evaporated, for contradictory reasons: one, I was too busy to while away the hours, and two, the golf course had little appeal when I was thinking about the activity in the Singspiration office going on without me.

The Lord kept trying to break through with signals of reassurance. Marie and I attended a church in Phoenix whose guest preacher was a missionary to the Navaho Indians. Just before the sermon his wife sang my song "Jesus Led Me All the Way." She did not know we were in the congregation, nor could she know the song was a sorely needed message at the moment. I thanked God for it, and my spirits lifted temporarily. But soon I was sunk in gloom once more.

It went on for months, almost as if in self-pity I had shut myself off from the grace and comfort of God. I hadn't, actually. In my private devotions He would continually speak to me through the Bible. And Sunday after Sunday in church a gifted young preacher was channeling God's grace to me so strongly through his sermons that I would sometimes go home and weep for joy. But on Monday morning my depression would return.

Where was my reliance on the idea of the planned life — the conviction that God had ordained each step of my journey for purposes of His own and would produce good works through me if I remained obedient? When I had considered stepping down as head of the company, I had prayed, *Lord, if this isn't in Your will, hit me over the head and stop me.* He hadn't stopped me. Yet here I was, stewing, unable to rise above my depression and accept God's clear-cut assurances and comfort.

Time came to my rescue. Time, Marie, and work.

One major composition after another came to life as I scribbled away in my quiet study or sat at the piano. *The Good Life, Jesus Is Coming, King of Kings, The Last Week, Christ Is Born* — bringing to more than twenty the number of full-length musicals and cantatas I had produced. Plus, of course, many new songs.

Requests for personal appearances kept pouring in, and I was again faced with the problem of which ones to accept. It was good to be in that harness; I loved the choral workshops and conducting appearances and soon built up a complicated travel schedule once more. My health was much improved, but I guarded it with vigilance, especially when traveling or in situations that called for a great expenditure of effort and energy.

The depression passed, finally, and I began to enjoy to the full my time alone with Marie in our house on the side of the mountain. Once I had relaxed and accepted the change in my routine, a great weight rolled off my back and I could luxuriate in work and in my many blessings.

The girls had remained in the Grand Rapids area when Marie and I moved to Arizona. We knew that our time spent with them would be drastically cut, but they were adults with their own lives to lead, and we never doubted they would keep in close touch or visit us as often as possible. Candy worked for several years as secretary to John Miles, president of the Grand Rapids School of the Bible and Music, before her marriage to Rodger Strader. Sandi and Pam shared an apartment; Sandi worked in the offices of Singspiration while Pam pursued additional studies and wrote songs, until Sandi found her life's partner in a young schoolteacher named Tom Catzere.

At that point Pam, our youngest, joined us in Arizona as my official but highly valued assistant. It signaled the eventual reuniting of the Peterson family, for later on Candy and Rodger also moved to Phoenix where he got a teaching job and worked toward an academic degree. The circle was complete when Sandi and Tom decided to go house-hunting in Phoenix with the plan that Tom would become my administrative assistant, business manager, and general factotum.

Not so incidentally, Candy and Rodger initiated Marie and me into the ranks of grandparents with the birth of Andrew John Strader in the summer of 1974 and Jennifer Marie Strader a year later. Whenever I leave on a trip or return home, Candy brings Andrew to the airport. He really likes his grandpa, and of course that pleases me immensely. It's hard for me to think of Marie as a grandma, though, for in my eyes she's still as young and beautiful as on our wedding day more than thirty years ago.

It all seems such a miracle — our coming together as a family again; the acceptance of my music which never seems to slacken; the traveling and conducting; the continued growth of Singspiration; the friendships that go on and on — with Pat Zondervan and so many others, in Grand Rapids and across the nation; the sparks of musical genius I see in Pam and

Rodger; the fact that my daughters are now working together as a trio again; their plans — with Tom and Rodger — for a new music publishing company that have taken shape; the bewitching sparkle in Andrew's eyes when I come home weary and he reaches out his arms to me. All wonderful. All, to some degree, miraculous!

Meanwhile, I press on with the next task at hand. There are lyrics to shape, music to write, engagements to fulfill, people to pray for, challenges to meet.

There are also some extra blessings — like winning SESAC's International Gospel Songwriting Award for 1975, or riding in a White House limousine to the airport after meeting and chatting with the President of the United States, or receiving a letter from President Ford expressing his appreciation for *I Love America* (one of my treasured mementos).

And sometimes at night I gaze up at the stars gleaming over Arizona — the ageless stars that stirred my soul as I flew over the Himalayas so many years ago; the same stars that have studded the heavens since creation itself — and I'm overwhelmed with wonder.

The calendar and the mirror don't lie, but somehow almighty God keeps me starry-eyed, with the same zest for life, the same childlike faith He honored when I had to trust Him for eleven cents to ride the Chicago el. In my heart I'm still the Kansas boy kneeling at the foot of the cross and finding salvation. Still the youngster dazzled by the magnitude of God's creation revealed in the shattering power of a storm over the mountaintops of Asia. Still the earnest young man with a passion to give the world a song — a song to the glory of God.

The miracle goes on.